UNTAPPED RICHES

UNTAPPED RICHES

Never Pay Off Your Mortgage—
and Other Surprising Secrets
for Building Wealth

Susan and Anthony Cutaia
with Robert Slater

AMACOM
American Management Association
New York • Atlanta • Brussels • Chicago • Mexico City • San Francisco
Shanghai • Tokyo • Toronto • Washington, D.C.

Special discounts on bulk quantities of AMACOM books are
available to corporations, professional associations, and other
organizations. For details, contact Special Sales Department,
AMACOM, a division of American Management Association,
1601 Broadway, New York, NY 10019.
Tel: 212-903-8316. Fax: 212-903-8083.
E-mail: specialsls@amanet.org
Website: www.amacombooks.org/go/specialsales
To view all AMACOM titles go to: www.amacombooks.org

This publication is designed to provide accurate and authoritative
information in regard to the subject matter covered. It is sold with the
understanding that the publisher is not engaged in rendering legal,
accounting, or other professional service. If legal advice or other expert
assistance is required, the services of a competent professional person
should be sought.

REALTOR® is a registered collective membership mark that identifies a
real estate professional who is a member of the National Association of
REALTORS® and subscribes to its strict Code of Ethics. AMACOM uses
these names throughout this book in initial capital letters or ALL
CAPITAL letters for editorial purposes only, with no intention of
trademark violation.

The authors wish to state that all numbers—interest rates, monthly
mortgage payment, etc.—are valid as of the middle of 2006 but may
have changed by the time of publication of this book because rates and
terms are subject to change without notice. The authors also wish to state
that we use the phrase "New Smart Loan™" to indicate the special kind
of smart loan that we offer clients. We have trademarked the phrase
"New Smart Loan™." In a few cases, we employ the phrase "smart loan"
when we refer to the program generically.

Library of Congress Cataloging-in-Publication Data

Cutaia, Anthony.
      Untapped riches : never pay off your mortgage—and other surprising secrets for
building wealth / Anthony and Susan Cutaia ; with Robert Slater.
         p.   cm.
      Includes bibliographical references and index.
      ISBN-10: 0-8144-7396-2
      ISBN-13: 978-0-8144-7396-2
      1. Real estate investment—United States.   2. Residential real estate—
United States.   3. House buying—United States.   4. House selling—
United States.   I. Cutaia, Susan.   II. Slater, Robert, 1943– .
III. Title.
HD259.C88   2007
332.63'24—dc22   2006019265

Printing number

10   9   8   7   6   5   4   3   2   1

Contents

Preface:

A Message from Anthony Cutaia

At the age of 21 in the early 1970s I joined Edwards and Hanley in New York City, entering their training program to learn to become a stockbroker. I chose to be proactive from the very start. I did not want to just sit around, as others were doing, and wait for a great stock to leap out at me. That hardly seemed the right approach. Instead, I decided that I would learn as much as I could on my own so that I could show people what some of the better investment vehicles were.

Yet, even that approach turned out to be haphazard and chancy. I needed to develop a financial planning strategy. Along the way I grew to appreciate the concept of the "timeliness of money." What did that phrase mean? It meant that there was a good time to make a move on the financial front as well as a bad time. And I had better learn the difference as early as possible.

A Conservative in Finances

I began my career as something of a conservative when it came to finances, believing that simply by conserving cash in accounts that provided compound interest one possessed a very powerful tool in building wealth. I still believe in these principles today, 30 years later, only now I am pushing it to the next level.

I did not want to see people "bury" their cash in equity then; I do not want to see them do it today. Putting your cash in equity means putting all of your cash into the hands of the banks.

I want people to have cash at their disposal so that they can use it to build wealth.

What I've done today in our business is to take the principles that I used 30 years ago and shift them to the next level by arguing that you should use the equity that exists in your investment vehicles as a catalyst or "feeder" to build additional wealth.

The investment vehicles of today may be different, they could be an annuity or mutual fund or some other kind of transaction, but the basic concept—the timeliness of money—is as important today as it was in the past. You have got to know when it is the right time to make a move on the financial front—and when it is the wrong time.

In the early years I used to call this notion "dollar cost averaging" and I had people make investments every month in mutual funds. That was the philosophy that was promulgated at that time. Some followed it; some did not.

When I got into mortgages and real estate, I began to see that I was doing things that were the natural extensions of the things I had been doing earlier. Now, as properties appreciate in value, still using the concept of the time use of money, my wife and business partner Susan Cutaia and I urge our clients, the new class of real estate investors, to look upon their investment vehicles as a means to accumulate wealth.

The investment vehicle thus becomes the "feeder" of one's overall investment strategy: the idea is to use real estate to take out equity and convert it into real cash. That is what this book is all about.

ANTHONY CUTAIA

Introduction

In earlier days, when we thought of a real estate professional, it was usually someone who dealt mostly in commercial real estate; who bought and sold large-sized projects—malls and skyscrapers and the like; someone who turned over scores of properties quickly and profitably. This professional made real estate his or her main occupation.

Today, thanks to the boom in real estate, a new class is emerging, a class of "budding professionals," as we like to call them: average people, often with regular day jobs, who regard property as a marvelous investment and want to become regulars in the buying and selling of real estate.

We see them every day in our real estate and mortgage business. Indeed, they are the lifeblood of what we do. Possibly cardiologists or television producers, used car sellers or handymen, they may be wealthy or simply comfortable.

Today many do not aspire to be true real estate professionals (what cardiologist would?), but some, perhaps as a way of sliding gently into retirement, just might want to abandon their day jobs. For now they want to buy and sell real estate as often as is sensible and feasible.

What has aided them enormously is an entirely new set of mortgage instruments and real estate strategies that allows real estate investors to think about purchasing more than just one property. These are programs that we favor. These are programs that we have researched and made an important part of our arsenal. These are programs that will almost certainly have a positive impact on your lives. We get into these programs in much greater detail later on in the book.

In the past we could never have provided this much guidance to the average person, for a very good reason. Even if they were interested in doing real estate transactions, most people have held back from getting involved in real estate, never quite knowing how or where to start. They have found the subjects of real estate and mortgages complicated, remote, and far too abstruse with which to get involved.

Getting the Right Advice

But real estate investors are much more savvy now. They are increasingly confident that they can get good, solid advice. More and more, they know where to turn to get that advice. We are writing this book for this group of real estate enthusiasts, potential and existing.

In *Untapped Riches*, we try to direct these enthusiasts into the fruitful world of profit making.

If the mortgage and real estate field were simple, if anyone could pick up the basics in a few hours, there would be no need for advice. But the subject has become vastly complicated with the advent of a set of mysterious, complex mortgage and real estate instruments.

There are lots of questions that new investors are going to have surrounding these instruments; that's why we thought it timely for us to produce this book and thus provide the first systematic look at these new ways of buying and selling real estate and at the same time creating wealth.

The main advice given in these pages is how to create wealth.

The goal is to show the new class of real estate investors how to become dynamic, profit-taking activists.

The strategies elaborated here give an incentive to look carefully at mortgage programs that you may have never heard of and certainly had not considered before reading these pages. We've given you a rundown of some of the most enticing and rewarding real estate instruments.

The ongoing real estate boom has created the incentive for you to get involved in real estate and mortgages with the same zeal that we in the business feel. Because there are so many properties coming on the market and the market itself is dynamic and moving so much of the time, it is the perfect moment to get involved. Five or six years ago, you may well have been holding a piece of property that was worth $150,000. Now that same property has ballooned to $500,000. What an incentive to become a real estate player.

With so many properties appreciating in like fashion, it is not surprising that many people say to themselves: wouldn't it be great if I could get a hold of a number of real estate properties? I could make some decent money from this boom.

Some began doing just this.

Lacking the capital or ambition or know-how to buy malls or skyscrapers, and uneager to devote the time required to take on projects of such magnitude, new investors began small, scooping up single-family homes, purchasing as few as two or three properties at first; they then began to graduate to multifamily homes, small strip centers, and then moved on ultimately to condominiums and neighborhood shopping centers; sometimes even to commercial real estate.

Those investors who buy and sell real estate for less than 750 hours a year have become the fastest growing segment of the buying and selling side of the real estate business. They are, of course, not the only people who want to invest in real estate.

As owners of one of the most successful real estate and mortgage companies in Florida, and as the proponents of strategies that have particular appeal to new real estate investors, we find these people, happily for us, flocking to our office every day. Although they are looking for information and guidance, they have several important traits in common:

- They believe that the ideal way to invest their money is in real estate (rather than the stock or bond markets).
- They want to make money, and they want it now!
- They are hungry for advice on how to get their feet wet or on how to build even greater wealth from real estate and mortgages.

They're not like professional real estate developers, who know how to get millions of dollars of financing from financial institutions at the drop of a hat. These are people who have worked hard for years, saved some money, and at one time or another, had most of their cash tied up as equity in a home, a home that may be worth a small fortune today, but provides no usable cash for the present.

For that, they need good advice.

To whom should they turn: the banks, other financial institutions, real estate brokers, or so-called experts on the Internet? Investors, in fact, should turn to none of these. People from a bank or the Internet can be quite the experts on all of the traditional ways to deploy mortgages. They can be quite adept at providing what they consider the simplest and the safest ways to create a mortgage. But none of them can talk with any authority on all the new mortgage instruments available, on the best ways to keep a high credit rating, or on what properties are coming on the market. While the banks and even the new voices on the Internet feel an obligation to offer these new mortgage instruments, these traditionalists are not great enthusiasts of these new approaches to mortgages. That means they are not the best people to promote such arrangements. They may have become experts on one of the new programs but they certainly do not have a grasp of all of them. That is where we come in.

With so much to say to early-stage real estate pros, we want to put our strategies before them with the hope that they will quickly benefit. Though no way exists to say how many potential real estate investors exist, we guess that they number in the hundreds of thousands across the nation and that number is growing every day.

We have an underlying philosophy toward real estate and mortgages that is fundamentally different from most of these other folks. We want to put cash into your pocket. We don't think that debt is such a bad thing. Most important, our methods work. They lead to wealth creation.

We have a set of beliefs that can often be summarized in just a few words. These beliefs are what we are all about. They also serve to distinguish us from all the others. For instance, we note "cash is king." And we urge you to "minimize your mortgage payment" and "maximize the use of leverage and the use of compound interest." Finally, we urge you to "pay yourself first before you pay the bank."

To help you implement these beliefs, we articulate throughout the book a set of strategies that we utilize and that work for us. We hope you will adapt some if not all as you learn the ins and outs of becoming a real estate pro.

UNTAPPED
RICHES

PART I

CHANGING
PERSPECTIVE

CHAPTER 1

Never Pay Off Your Mortgage

STRATEGY #1:
CONVERT THE "DEAD MONEY" YOU HAVE IN HOME
EQUITY INTO USABLE CASH.

Investing in real estate is exciting and can bring huge returns. But, especially if you are new to the game, you have to be careful about how you allocate funds. By following conventional advice, you may have been making a profound and costly mistake in how you dispose of your money. This all-too-common mistake is in transforming all of your potentially usable cash into equity in your home.

Sadly, most people have taken the wrong advice from the wrong people—people who work for banks and financial institutions, who seemed trustworthy and smart but who have placed the banks' interests above that of their client's.

The banks and financial institutions had it their way for many years. When it came to mortgages, they set the rules. They decided what was good for you. They urged on you mortgage strategies that were designed to help the banks, not investors. They promoted the values that worked best for them, not for investors. They did all this by choosing which mortgage instruments to make available.

No one complained. No one asked if there was a better way of doing things. People went along because—quite frankly—they didn't know any better. After all bank officials dressed nicely, they were young and energetic, they sounded as if they knew what they were talking about. How could one question their advice?

The banks were suggesting that a mortgage had one and only one purpose—and that was to help the borrower pay off the debt on a home conveniently, taking as long as 15 to 30 years to become debt free.

The banks did not think of a mortgage as the driver of wealth creation—as putting usable cash in the pockets of borrowers. That was the last thing on their minds. The banks advised borrowers to pay off their mortgages quickly—and to seek profits, via usable cash, in other investment vehicles only *after* a mortgage was paid off.

It seemed like good, safe advice. But what it meant was that many borrowers were swallowing whole the bank's philosophy that it was better to have cash tomorrow rather than to have cash today.

What the banks should have been doing was to help people accumulate their own ready-to-use cash. Instead they have done a magnificent job of convincing future real estate investors to turn over their hard-earned income to the banks in the form of enormously high mortgage payments. The size of a mortgage payment depends on how much one borrows (the principal), the length of the loan (its maturity or term), and the interest rate.

It has been the banks that have propagated the belief that you should pay down a mortgage as quickly as possible so that, in older age, you do not have to make monthly mortgage payments. We are not at all sympathetic to such a strategy because it leaves you with very little disposable cash with which to create greater wealth.

Because the banks and other financial institutions have convinced so many people of the wisdom of paying off their mortgages quickly, it is important to spell out why it is so important to have cash in your pocket. For years people paid off their mortgages instead of asking whether it wouldn't be better to have cash available for immediate use. And there are indeed a number of reasons that ready cash is so important.

First of all, the more cash that you have available now, the easier it is for you to purchase items, whether it is food at the grocery store or a piece of real estate. Just as important, the more cash that you have in your pocket, the easier it is to leverage that cash into even larger sums of cash. If you have no cash flow, it would not be possible to build up millions of dollars in value.

By increasing your cash position you can buy more investment property, put more money aside in interest-bearing accounts, and get into the stock market. You can look for better financial terms and more mortgage options.

With all the advantages now afforded both from the banks (who offer compound interest on their accounts) and from the wealth creation that is inherent in real estate appreciation, it simply makes no sense to pour what we call "dead money" into monthly mortgage payments.

The money that is poured into these payments is "dead" because it is not available for the creation of cash flow and investment. It can of course be accessed theoretically whenever the owner wants to refinance or sell. If the owner sells the property, he or she relinquishes any and all equity in the property. The main point—and people have a hard time understanding this—is that putting the money in other investments will yield more than if the money is used to pay off the mortgage.

Investors should look for advice from those who provide it across the whole gamut of real estate and mortgages. They should look for specialists like ourselves who can suggest ways for the real estate investors to convert the dead money they have ill-advisedly put into home equity, into usable cash.

Here's a practical example of a fellow who came into our office, hoping to refinance some of his properties. We showed him how to convert his dead money into usable cash.

We had refinanced one of his properties about three and a half years earlier. The value of that property was $210,000. Back then he had taken out a $168,000 mortgage on the property with a monthly payment of $786, which was at a pay rate of 3.83%.

But now, when we looked at his situation—taking into account the appreciation in value to $467,000 on his properties—we drew up a new mortgage for $374,000 with a monthly mortgage payment of $945.

The man told us that he owned some other properties on which he had a home equity line. He wanted to extract some money from these properties in order to invest in a business. But he was reluctant to draw down his equity line because the rates had been far more volatile on this line than on other mortgage instruments that he was starting to hear about. We advised him that his reluctance was well founded, that he was quite right not to draw down on the equity line.

We set up a new mortgage arrangement for him. And because of that, he had been able to take $200,000 out of his property (what was left of the $374,000 left him with $206,000 less closing costs as a result of the new mortgage amount). The new mortgage was done within 30 days. If he had been building a new business or making an investment and had needed to act quickly, our advice to him would have been to draw down on the equity line. But because the interest rates on the equity line are so volatile, our advice was that he convert that line of credit into a better mortgage instrument, one that had a less volatile index and had better payment options.

What were some of those better payment options? Chief among them is the "smart loan." The smart loan is a loan that provides for four payment options: a minimum payment option; an interest only payment option; a 15-year amortized payment option; and a 30-year amortized payment option. The loan is "smart" because it provides flexibility through these options.

If our client took an interest-only loan, he would pay only $1,083 a month as a mortgage payment. A minimum-payment loan would require him to pay $505 a month in mortgage payments. Thus, it would be to his advantage to take a smart loan, especially if he is setting up a new business, because he would have to pay less per month—either $505 a month or $1,083 a month. If the person took that same $200,000 with a 6% interest rate over a 15-year term, the monthly mortgage payment would be $1,687, obviously a much worse position.

The man who had come into our office really liked the "smart loan" options. He was smart to follow advice about these options. You should follow another piece of advice as well: Before you think about buying a piece of property, explore what your options are; find out how much in monthly mortgage payments you will have to make. Project it out for five years. That's a long enough projection because you will probably want to refinance within that period.

We told him there was a very good possibility that he would want to refinance in the not-too-distant future; by doing so, after all, he would be able to take more cash out of the property.

Why Refinance?

Start with the fact that at this particular time property prices are rather dramatically appreciating on an annual basis; at times there is appreciation on a monthly basis. So it makes a great deal of sense to think about refinancing after five years, perhaps even after three years.

Another advantage of refinancing is this: within the mortgage instrument that we use, at the end of five years, the program goes over to a fully indexed rate. At that point the monthly payment could increase, but not necessarily.

It would make sense then for the borrower to go back to the original monthly payment, by using either the minimum payment or the "smart loan" program.

With both the pay rate and the interest rate continuing to drop, you have the opportunity to lower your mortgage payments and increase the amount of cash you are taking out of the property by refinancing. You could then take that money and do something else with it.

STRATEGY #2:
USE LEVERAGE TO CREATE WEALTH.

As we like to say, there is "good" debt and "bad" debt.

Of course some would say all debt is bad. In some respects we might agree with that, but we're aware that "good" debt enables you to create wealth.

The one advantage you have in a real estate transaction is that real estate can appreciate in value.

It's leverage that makes money for you. If you do not use leverage in a real estate transaction, you might as well go buy a bond because it's the leverage that increases your return on investment and increases your yield.

Here's an example that will show why it makes sense to use leverage and why it's better to have cash in your pocket—rather than have your hard-earned income tied up in equity in a long-term mortgage.

If you have a $200,000 property, which you can rent for $16,000 a year (without taxes and insurance), it is generating an 8% return on your investment. Not a bad return, right?

But if you take the same $200,000 property and get a 75% mortgage ($150,000) by using the New Smart Loan™ program that we employ a great deal in our business, you would have a minimum pay rate of 1.75% based on a 30-year amortization. This means that you will have to pay $535 in monthly payments, or $6,420 annually.

The property in our example generates $16,000 in rentals, and is now costing you $6,420 in mortgage payments. That means it's generating a net of $9,580 a year (without taxes and insurance).

But, since you would have only $50,000 invested in the property (the amount you would pay to obtain the $200,000 mortgage) and were getting this nearly $10,000 return, the return on your investment would be almost 20%. By leveraging your property, you have increased the yield from 8% to 20%.

So which is better?

It is clearly better to have the $200,000 cash in your pocket. With that $200,000 in cash, you could, in addition to spending $50,000 on the first $200,000 property, invest $150,000 for three more properties ($50,000 each), and you would have a grand total of $800,000 in real estate equity from the four properties ($200,000 per property)—generating nearly $40,000 in income.

That is a far better outcome than simply paying $200,000 directly for the $200,000 piece of property and having no mortgage to pay.

Hopefully it is now easier to understand why it is better to have cash in your pocket, and why it's of no value whatsoever to pour money into long-term fixed mortgages.

Investors can only benefit by shifting their investing strategy away from building equity toward creating cash flow. Paying off the mortgage deprives the investor of large quantities of cash flow. None of the $800,000 in value that is mentioned above would be available to investors who simply pay off their mortgages. The investor loses all that potential income by not capitalizing on cash flow.

Having said all this, it becomes self-evident why we propose the next strategy.

STRATEGY #3:
KEEP YOUR MONEY OUT OF THE BANK'S HANDS. NEVER PAY OFF YOUR MORTGAGE—NEVER!

This sounds like radical advice; and it's certainly not what most people hear from their advisers at the banks and other financial institutions. But it is perhaps the most important advice that can be given to real estate investors.

People look at such strategies and argue that they are imposing heavy risk on people. But there is risk in everything that one does—especially when it comes to investing and trying to create wealth. The only real way to avoid risk is not to invest.

What we offer is a way to generate usable cash. As part of that process we identify the risks and then help new real estate investors adopt strategies to manage the risk. We help them protect their principal while maximizing profit on as much of a tax-deferred basis as possible. The more money that can be freed up, the more managed the risk will be.

Once you accept this point of view, you are ready to move on to bigger and better things. You need to think long term, to plan not just the first transaction but future transactions.

Real estate is a great investment because it has one trait that no other investment possesses: it is not perishable. With real estate, it's possible to extract the equity built into it—and yet hold on to the asset and retain the value of the asset. Extracting equity means to take out the equity, reaffirming the fact that once the equity is sold, it's gone. Stocks and bonds don't allow for that.

To extract the equity of a stock or bond, you must sell it, and once it's sold, that's it; it's gone, and you don't own it any more. That's what makes real estate the best way to invest.

STRATEGY #4:
FIND A MORTGAGE FIRST, THEN FIND THE PROPERTY.

Here's a strategy that may seem unorthodox, but makes great sense: find the mortgage before the property. Many real estate specialists insist on locating a piece of property for a client first and only then searching around for a mortgage. But, one does not need to own a property to secure the loan. The property is really the last thing you need; what you need to know is what kind of mortgage you qualify for and you can find that out even before locating a property.

You could find a property first—but then it could take a long time to go through the approval process, whereas you can be approved for a specific amount of money based on becoming qualified in a relatively short amount of time. The financing is based on one's credit and one's ability to make the monthly payments. It is not based entirely on the value of the property.

One disadvantage of finding the property prior to securing the mortgage: You could become qualified to purchase a property for $1 million but could decide ultimately only to purchase a property worth $200,000.

If your credit is not good, greater attention is paid to what you own by way of real estate; and you are going to wind up with a much lower loan to value and a much higher interest rate.

You must find a mortgage first, the best possible mortgage that works best for you; it will be the mortgage that goes hand in hand with your qualifications. Finding the right mortgage is crucial. It must be a mortgage that allows the investor to free up lots of usable cash. That means finding a mortgage in which the monthly payments are as low as possible.

Make Sure Your Credit Is in Order

Being financially creditworthy is important. It does not do you much good to have a great income and good assets if you have a poor credit score.

Credit scoring is tough. Sometimes simply checking one's credit can pull the credit score down. That can really add up if multiple sources are requesting credit checks on you. If you signed on to a mortgage company, and you gave them your Social Security number, that would provide them the opportunity at their discretion to look at your credit. Those inquiries count against you. They can pull your credit score down.

The people who do credit scoring have some pretty strict rules. With a 681 credit score you could qualify for certain mortgage programs but you could easily dip below that figure, losing 20 points if you made one credit card payment late.

We recommend that you try to get these inquiries wiped off the books by writing to the credit-reporting agency and challenging the inquiry. Sometimes these companies don't really have specific authorization to request a credit report. It is important that your mortgage broker work with a credit repair company to fight with the credit companies on your behalf.

We once had the owner of a carpet store as well as a fleet of trucks come into the office. He had gotten his credit scores up and had found just the mortgage that he wanted. But his credit was challenged because each time he bought a new truck the car dealer gave his Social Security number to 20 lenders as part of the effort to secure financing for him.

The effect of all these inquiries was to lower his credit score again.

We advised the carpet store owner to work with a bank with which he does business rather than with the car dealer. The bank will be the only one pulling the carpet store owner's credit, while the car dealer is going to shop the loan to many banks. It is quite possible that the loans are being shopped to the bank the carpet store owner does business with in the first place.

People usually don't know what their credit score is. They will still insist that their credit is excellent. They brush off their problems by saying, "Oh, I have just a few lates." But each of those "lates" probably cost them 30 points of their credit score. The public unfortunately doesn't have a true idea of how important credit scores are to obtaining a mortgage.

CHAPTER 2

Don't Be House Rich and Cash Poor

We will soon turn to the newly created mortgage and real estate programs that should have a powerful and positive impact on your finances. But first we want to explain why new investors have had such a hard time taking advantage of these programs before now.

For a long time, anyone with pretensions of becoming a real estate investor had been trapped in the old-school way of thinking: everyone advised him or her to pay off a mortgage as quickly as possible. That meant turning over his or her cash to the banks or financial institutions, leaving the person with little or no usable cash. They were making a higher monthly mortgage payment, and not leveraging their money to make more money.

Without usable cash, it was impossible for the investor to think about purchasing real estate on a continuing basis. Without usable cash, the investor could not exploit the new mortgage and real estate vehicles.

Then came the boom in real estate—and new investors were raring to go. They wanted to capitalize on that boom. To do that, of course, they needed cash.

The explosion in the real estate market in our home state of Florida the past few years has been unprecedented. No one has ever seen such interest in real estate. The state has issued 295,000 real estate licenses. There are thousands of real estate agents in southern Florida. The market is truly at an all-time high. It seems that everyone has developed an interest in real estate.

Low interest rates coupled with an extremely attractive life-style have caused the real estate boom in southern Florida. Prices have skyrocketed and the average cost of a home in Palm Beach County has risen to $406,000 (compared to 2001 when the price for a home was "only" $250,000).

The soaring prices have exposed an intriguing conundrum for those who bought a house years ago.

Someone purchasing a $150,000 home ten years ago, relying on a $75,000 mortgage to pay off the home, now finds that his or her home is worth $500,000. The equity in that home has appreciated dramatically and the owner may well have already paid off the $75,000 mortgage or a good portion of it.

Meanwhile, the person has accumulated $425,000 of equity that is simply sitting there and doing nothing.

This person is a classic example of what we mean by being house rich and cash poor.

As long as such people cling to the wrong-headed mortgage strategy of putting "dead money" into the equity in their homes, they are going to be unable to take advantage of the newly created mortgage and real estate instruments that will be explained in great detail later in this book.

Imagine someone carrying a package of $100 bills, taking the package home, emptying it at home, and then stuffing the bills in a hole in the backyard—instead of investing it. Without knowing much about the person, it would be easy to ascribe some serious mental illness to him or her. Why would anyone voluntarily put so much money in a hole in the ground, making it impossible to earn any money on the cash they are socking away?

Well, that's the equivalent of what the old-school folks who are paying off their mortgages as fast as possible are doing. Until now many people kept their "savings" in home mortgages that yielded no cash at all.

These folks had been told that they must strive to become debt free. But no one has told them how dire the consequences of pursuing old-school ways are. No one has tried to stop these people from doing the equivalent of stuffing a great deal of money in a hole in the ground. The goal of this book is to stop these people from doing just that.

Recently, we had a retired gentleman and his daughter come to our offices looking for our advice on mortgages. Here is their story:

He had a generous retirement plan from a pharmaceutical firm, and he wanted to buy a condo that he had found. Had the market been better, he could have cashed out his retirement plan (for $750,000), but the market had dropped and it made no sense for him to touch the plan. Instead, his daughter lent him $450,000 to buy the condo, but she later said that she needed the $450,000 back. The father knew that it would make little sense for him to take the cash out of the retirement plan because he would be exercising his shares at a much lower value than if he were to wait until the value rose. He also had a small mortgage above and beyond the $450,000 that he had invested in the condo.

After listening to us on the radio, the man and his daughter visited us in our offices. She wanted to refinance into a 15-year fixed rate mortgage. She could give no good reason for doing that other than to say that, "We'll pay it off faster."

We asked her: why would you want to do that? We told her that as long as she can have manageable monthly payments it made no sense to take out a 15-year fixed rate mortgage. We suggested that they turn to other kinds of mortgage instruments, where they would not have to use up their valuable income—and in a much shorter time they would have what they needed to pay off the mortgage.

We suggested that they take a "New Smart Loan™" and cash out the stock options when the options rose in value. Even if the stock options did not rise in value, it was better for them to take a minimum-payments mortgage than to take a 15-year fixed mortgage, burying the money in the bank in much the same way that someone might bury money in their backyard. By burying in their backyard, the money cannot be converted to cash any more than it could if it is turned over to the bank in the form of monthly mortgage payments.

Why would anyone voluntarily bury his or her money in the backyard?

The best advice to give these people is: stop "burying" your money in a bank. Your money is not earning new cash. Indeed, it is losing value: the greater the inflation, the less buying power you have.

Clinging to the Old School

Who or what is driving these people to that "hole" in the backyard? It is the banks and other financial institutions that are the culprits, urging on clients mortgage payment strategies that are the equivalent of socking their cash away without any chance of wealth creation.

The clients socked their cash away in all innocence. It was not as if someone had explained to them their choices and they made a conscious decision to go down one path and not another. But now we're telling you, there's a better way.

STRATEGY #5:
STOP THINKING THAT BEING DEBT FREE IS GOOD.

Spurred on by the banks, new investors mistakenly thought that becoming debt free was desirable. They owned homes that were sometimes worth millions and certainly hundreds of thousands of dollars but they had no disposable cash—making for an absurd situation.

They were the classic house-rich and cash-poor victims of the old school way of thinking about mortgages. And, to make matters worse, they have been making this mistake for years. In the early years, when there was something they could have done to improve their situation, no one explained to them how to invest their money more wisely.

That was really a shame. Because, in those early years they had the money and the earning power and thus could have saved money in a cash instrument.

But they got bad advice, and so they put their money into non-cash items, especially fixed term mortgage instruments. As they reach their golden years, these homeowners no longer qualify for mortgages that could ease them out of their house-rich and cash-poor dilemma. They could get cash, of course—by selling their property, or by doing a reverse mortgage—but these were hardly optimal solutions. (A reverse mortgage is a mortgage loan on which the debt of the borrower increases over time; but the debt does not have to be repaid until the borrower dies, or sells the house, or moves out permanently.)

If you want to build equity in your investments, how much better off you would be to build equity in a home without spending your own earnings to pay down the mortgage. How much

better you would be if you could build equity simply by letting
your investment appreciate in value

Enshrining a Sacred Value

The banks and financial institutions have enshrined as a sacred
value the notion that everyone should be debt free. The only way
to do that, they insist, is to pay down a mortgage as quickly as
possible until the balance is zero. Only then, say the banks, does
it make sense to seek to extract profit from a property. Oh how
the banks love it when this strategy is followed.

Banks sometimes even offer a mortgage acceleration payment
plan so that someone can make a payment twice a month, helping
to knock a few years off the mortgage. Nothing makes a bank
happier than if someone joins this plan.

The borrower weeps with joy—and why not? After all, the
bank was merely helping the borrower to cut short the mortgage.
The bank seemed to be doing a big favor. But it was not—because
the borrower was paying down the mortgage with hard-earned
dollars that could have been put to better use elsewhere.

The banks also convinced everyone that the most secure place
for one's "cash" was in a mortgage program in a bank. Then the
banks threw in that borrowers could be free and clear of mortgage
debt in a mere 15 years, making the idea sound most appealing.
But being debt free doesn't help you build wealth. It just locks
up your money in equity.

STRATEGY #6:
LET THE MONTHLY MORTGAGE PAYMENT DETERMINE
YOUR CHOICE OF MORTGAGE, NOT INTEREST RATES.

Banks often take the narrow view that clients should be mostly
concerned with which mortgages carry low interest rates. Banks

act as if interest rates should be the only determining factor in selecting a mortgage, but that is not the way it should be.

Investors should think of the amount of the monthly mortgage payment as the key determinant and not the size of interest rates—because it's by making a small monthly payment that they will free up usable cash.

STRATEGY #7:
DEVELOP CLEAR-CUT OBJECTIVES FOR USING THE CASH YOU WILL DRAW OUT OF YOUR PROPERTY.

If you are interested in becoming a real estate investor, the first thing you should do is ask yourself why you want to extract cash from the equity in your home: paying children's college bills, relieving credit card debt, taking care of elderly parents. When you are sure there is a good reason to use the cash, then figure out how much you can extract.

Determining the Amount of Cash to Extract

The first step is to spell out your net worth. Begin by evaluating your home. That is likely to be your largest asset. The best way to determine the value of your home is to order an appraisal. You will also need to know, if there is a mortgage, how much is still owed on the property? What could you afford to pay into a saving plan from the money you saved?

You will need to look at your creditworthiness next. Where are you in your credit payments? Are you under water? That is, do you have too much debt compared to income?

Once it is clear what can be pulled out of the property, you should turn to a financial planner. The financial planner will determine the amount of money you can live on from month to month. So if you can bring in $1,000 a month in income from real estate and can generate another $2,000 in income from your day job, that should be fine. Here your employment history comes into the picture, at least in part, to help determine how much the person can pay in mortgage payments, and how much he or she can invest.

If your monthly income is $11,000, the rule of thumb is that your total debt including your mortgage, taxes, insurance, credit cards, and car payments should not exceed 36% of your monthly income—or $3,960 a month. You can purchase a home worth as much as $400,000.

The next step is to set up a mortgage arrangement.

Most people want to know how they will pay in monthly payments. If you want to pay the least amount in monthly mortgage payments, look at the "negative amortization" plan, one of the new mortgage instruments spelled out in this book in Chapters 9 and 10, where some interest is deferred. By going that route you will either save money or be able to pay off a credit card.

If you want usable cash, take some money from equity from your home because the home has appreciated in value. You may be able to pull out of the house as much as $200,000 or $300,000.

In most cases you can have a monthly income and still have sufficient dollars to service the debt of the new mortgage.

CHAPTER 3

Create the Ideal Exit Strategy

The primary goal in investing in real estate should be to convert the value of your property into cash. This conversion is known as an exit strategy. There are various exit strategies. Some convert money tied up in equity into cash, and some convert property into other property (performing a 1031 Exchange, for example). When you refinance that new property, you convert that property into cash, and reduce your taxes—all part of an exit strategy. Employing cost segregation analysis, i.e., using depreciation to reduce taxes, is another exit strategy. We will be talking about these exit strategies—1031 Exchanges and Cost Segregation Analysis—in greater detail in later chapters.

New investors need to think about exit strategies all the time.

STRATEGY #8:
LET YOUR PROPERTY APPRECIATE IN VALUE; THEN
EXTRACT (HARVEST) THE CASH FROM IT.

Real estate can be thought of as an "equity farm," because every time a property appreciates in value the borrower can extract the cash from that property, in effect "harvesting" the money and getting cash. That is an exit strategy.

This chapter talks about various optimal exit strategies in real estate—strategies that our investors have been using successfully for years.

You should think about why you are investing in the first place. You should think beyond the immediate moment. There are a lot of vehicles you can use to get into real estate. It is perhaps even more important to make sure you have a good plan for getting *out* of such an investment vehicle and converting your equity into a cash-producing venture. It's that cash that ultimately enables you to live better—or to just live!

Most people think of an exit strategy as coming up with optimal ways to sell something. But that is not the point. The real point is that you can retrieve your principal on a mortgage. More important, you can also make a profit by utilizing the usable cash from the equity that has been building up in your home mortgage.

Real estate affords numerous exit strategies that allow you to keep ownership of the asset—unlike stocks or bonds that require you to sell the asset, whatever it is, in order to realize or get back your money. The beauty of real estate is that you can retrieve your money, perhaps even make some profit—and not have to get rid of the asset.

Obviously the first exit strategy is the sale of a property.

The second exit strategy is the refinancing of a property.

The third would be incorporating the use of a 1031 Exchange. We devote an entire chapter to 1031 Exchanges later in the book.

(A variation of the third would be using a 1031 Exchange and refinancing the property to take cash out.)

A fourth exit strategy could be utilizing depreciation in order to shelter income generated from a property as part of detailed cost segregation studies, which are used to identify the components of a commercial transaction. There is a chapter later in the book on cost segregation studies.

Depreciation in Real Estate

One of the most misunderstood and most underutilized methods in real estate is depreciation.

What is depreciation? It's a non-cash loss. You can write that non-cash loss off against any income you have or against any passive income from other sources.

The objective in any real estate transaction is to create cash flow. And some of the ways that create cash flow are refinancing the property, having the property appreciate, or selling the property.

Let's say you have a property worth $350,000 and you have taken a loan for 90% of its value, $315,000. You can take that $315,000 of tax-free money and do whatever you want to do with it.

Now let's say the value of the property drops from $350,000 to $200,000.

Now what?

You don't have to make up the difference in loss unless you sell the property. In that sense, real estate is different from the stock market where you do have to repay the loss if you have taken a loan against the stock.

If the stock goes up from $20 to $50 and you take out $25, you just might have to repay the loan on the stock—you might have to repay $25.

Now let's say the stock goes from $50 to $25, prompting a

margin call. It's the worst call in the world. That phone rings and your secretary or someone says your broker is on the phone. You say, my broker who? My what? Tell him I'm not here.

If you don't come up with the cash to bring the margin call back into ratio, they sell the stock. So you automatically have created a tax loss. Great. This is what is called a real cash loss.

In the example above where you took $315,000 out of the $350,000 property, and the value of the property dropped to $200,000, so long as you are making your payments on that $315,000, you have a performing loan and that's it. They can't call the loan or force you to pay the difference, even if you have the cash on hand. There's nothing they can do about it as long as you keep the property.

If you sell the property at that point, then of course you have to pay off the difference, which could be substantial. But there's nothing that says you have to sell the property. You can weather that cycle.

What you've done is take cash out of the property as the property has been appreciating and converting that cash into other secured investments—and you still own the property!

Another example: You could take the money you pulled out of the property and buy more real estate at the new, depressed value. When the market turns itself around, you'll have two properties with incredible potential.

Real estate moves in cycles. It has done so, it seems, since there have been records that can be tracked. In today's world, real estate cycles seem to run every seven years. All you have to do is be patient.

In 1991 real estate was in the tank, lasting until 1995. Then the market started to come back.

People say the real estate market will go up forever: they are very mistaken. The one good thing about living to be 60 years old is that I've been through at least seven real estate cycles. If I live to be 89 I'll go through another four or five, because it is going to happen.

The point is that you have to think in the long term and take advantage of slow markets. You have to prepare. For ourselves and our clients, we prepared for the down cycle by making a conscious effort to move into other kinds of real estate, income-producing properties. We were in single family investment property, waterfront property, small and large professional buildings, small and large shopping centers. We continue to invest in income properties such as professional buildings and shopping centers.

Remember: it's the conversion of equity into cash—by refinancing or selling—that forms the exit strategy. Cash allows an independent person to live better or to just live. If you don't have an exit strategy, you can get stuck in that equity trap.

Most people have it upside down. They look to create equity in real estate and they want to have no debt on their property. The problem is that this is only part of the story. They should be trying to figure out how to convert their equity into cash. Then they should find ways to take that cash and put it into tax-deferred or tax-sheltered vehicles and use more of their money. Most people don't realize that they need to use more of their money to accumulate wealth.

Most are in a situation as we noted above, where when the stock market goes down, and a stock goes from 100 to 50, they now need to get a 100% return on their money. But it's a lot harder to get a 100% return on your money, i.e., to hope that the stock goes back to 100, than it is to get an 8% return on your money in the real estate field. For the 8%, the person needs to shelter cash, putting it into assets that can preserve capital.

It is just a matter of picking the right real estate. We buy and sell contracts on commercial properties and others can do the same thing. The problem is most don't know how to do it. They don't even understand how a contract is written. And they certainly don't understand how to sell that contract to someone else. These are the things we do and we do it all day long.

We tell our clients: You can't go into the real estate business with one eye open and one eye closed and half asleep. You have to use all of the tools available to you.

Before we look at the specific tools for helping one in developing exit strategies, we want to call your attention to a mistake that we hope you will learn to avoid.

CHAPTER 4

The Single Worst Mortgage in Creation: The Fixed Rate Mortgage

Banks should be educating everyone on how to turn mortgages into wealth creators. Instead, they advocate mortgages that have no wealth creation possibilities.

Banks have been advocating taking a 15-year or 30-year fixed rate mortgage as the safest and wisest course of action. The traditional fixed rate mortgage (FRM) has been the standard for many years. It became popular because neither the interest rate nor the monthly payment ever changed over the life of the loan. That allowed the borrower to know from the very beginning precisely how much a mortgage payment would be each month for the entire life of the loan.

For those who place a great value on predictability, the FRM offered just that—predictability and stability. But there was a price for this predictability—a higher interest rate. These longer loans cost more because of the total interest paid. For example, a

$50,000 loan for 30 years at 10% will have monthly payments of $438.79. That means that over 30 years, the borrower will have paid $107,964 in interest—more than twice the amount of the loan.

The same loan for 20 years would have monthly payments of $482.51 (an extra $44 per month), but the total interest paid will be only $65,802—a long-term savings of $42,162, if the borrower can afford the extra $44 per month.

Banks charge a higher rate of interest in order to offset the risk that at some point during the life of the loan interest rates will rise. Since the banks would not be allowed to raise the interest rate on your loan, according to the terms of that loan, the banks lower the risk of losing out on the profit from higher interest rates by charging a higher interest rate.

Still, it is fair to say that the FRM is the single worst mortgage in creation.

Why say this? First, because the only one that benefits is the banks. And second, because all you are doing is giving the bank your cash flow, year after year.

Free Money

The banks essentially get free money in the form of principal payments. Perhaps that is why these 15-year and 30-year fixed mortgages are increasingly in disfavor. Following our philosophy, you have to abhor all these long-range mortgages because, we believe, you should view your home as a wealth-building tool.

We run into the "victims" of the banks all the time. These are the people who own a home worth over $1 million and have barely enough money to buy food. Certainly you would think there was a happy solution for them. Unfortunately, however, for some of them this is not the case. Because of their age and their income level, they no longer qualify for the mortgage instruments as they would have when they were younger. In their younger years, when they had sufficient cash and earning power to save money and put it into a convertible cash instrument, they failed to take such a step.

As a result, in their later years they are unable to convert any of the equity they have built up into some kind of a cash item without doing a reverse mortgage, which we don't think is the best kind of mortgage instrument.

You'd be surprised how many people today have made very little preparation for their retirement and don't really know what to do. But they love the real estate boom and the possibilities that it holds out for them. They want to purchase as much property as possible. But they don't quite know how to do that.

They find the whole world of real estate complicated and they're not sure of where or how to invest their savings in that world. There's far more to real estate than simply buying into the latest condominium building and hoping to get out of the investment with some profit. If investors become part of that kind of herd mentality, they will get trampled.

STRATEGY #9:
WITH THE CASH YOU SAVE BY PAYING A LOWER MONTHLY MORTGAGE PAYMENT, LOOK FOR WEALTH-CREATION STRATEGIES THROUGH REAL ESTATE VENTURES.

People with a million dollars of equity in their homes but not enough cash to pay for their food must learn that the objective is not to pay off their debt. The objective is to have the amount of money needed to pay off the entire mortgage—but to use part of that money for wealth creation.

Think of your financial situation as a portrait of your assets and liabilities. If you have a lot of money stuck in equity, you have to consider that a liability. Your goal is to move some of the non-earning, illiquid assets from your liability column into your asset column, where your liquid, usable cash is listed.

So at the end of the day, when you look at the liability side, and it says you have $200,000 worth of debt and your asset side says you have the same $200,000, you can use the funds on the asset side to eliminate your debt at any time. That's a desirable position in which to find yourself, but it's not your real objective: your real objective is to leverage the money on the asset side into greater and greater wealth.

To fully appreciate how important it is to achieve a situation where you can have the assets available to create wealth, you have to understand the "time use of money." Once you understand that, you will be able to convert illiquid, non-earning equity into usable cash. The time use of money is the value over time of the money you use today. Evaluating the time use of money means taking into account taxes, inflation, compounding, and a bunch of other factors, especially the potential for leverage, when thinking about the use of money over a period of time.

We meet people all the time who keep pouring *all* of their cash into their homes. One person we met recently had a classic problem. He owned two pieces of property apart from his home. For the first he had paid $170,000 and it had climbed in value to $300,000. For the second he had paid $186,000 and its value had jumped to $280,000. He wanted to sell these two properties and use the proceeds to pay off his home, which was worth $500,000, and on which he owed $400,000.

We explained to him that that was the worst thing he could do.

His big problem was that he had equity in these two properties but he didn't have any cash. He was cash poor and house rich.

This is an issue for many people who are running out of cash. They start thinking about downsizing. They are holding properties that have great wealth, but that wealth is locked in and they can't put the money to work for them. For this client, selling the properties was not the answer. The answer was a different mortgage type, the kinds we explain in later chapters.

Cashing Out

Here's an example of another house-rich and cash-poor family: A couple owns a house that is now worth $500,000. It's totally paid off, although they are still paying taxes, insurance, and maintenance. They have little or no cash and came to us wanting to take cash out of the property. Their property has appreciated dramatically over the years, but they have never taken cash out of it.

They had a false sense of security, because their house is paid off. While they can claim a certain security, they have left themselves few financial opportunities. They have no real cash flow to help them take care of their normal living expenses. That's why they came to us. We set them up in one of our New Smart Loan™ programs, and they were grateful. Now they had money for their daily expenses. Soon they might be able to put enough money away for investment purposes. It was not too late for them to change their way of thinking and start leveraging their money.

With their home valued at $500,000 they were able to refinance for $400,000, with a monthly payment of $1,517. Now they have $400,000 available to themselves in cash. As long as they have a good credit rating, they have the opportunity to put that usable cash into one or more real estate opportunities.

STRATEGY #10:
MAKE MINIMUM MONTHLY MORTGAGE PAYMENTS AND NEVER MAKE EXTRA PAYMENTS.

A man named Eric phoned our television program one day recently to say that he had been advised to enter into a mortgage program that put an emphasis on reducing the mortgage debt by paying off his mortgage as quickly as possible through bimonthly payments. He had also heard that he might be able to do just as well if not better by putting some of his mortgage payment into some kind of savings account.

He was obviously not clear about which path to pursue.

We told him that in principle there was nothing wrong with the concept of debt reduction. Everyone should be looking for ways to reduce their overall debt. We are all in favor of reducing debt. But we also pointed out that there are two ways of achieving debt reduction: the right way (our way) and the wrong way (the bank's way). The wrong way, we told him, is to give money to the bank and let the bank earn money on your money, forcing you to lose the use of that money, and forcing you to lose the opportunity to have that money earn on a compounded basis.

Instead of making extra payments on the mortgage, it's better to get involved in one of the mortgage programs that we advocate and make minimum monthly mortgage payments. It's never a good idea to make extra payments on a bimonthly basis. Instead, if you have the extra money, put it into a savings or an investment account. You do not need to pay down that debt and you should use that money to accumulate wealth. So, at the end of 10 or 15 years, when you look at your personal balance sheet, your assets, and liabilities, you will have an asset column that is larger than your liability column. If instead you agree to the debt-reduction programs proposed by the banks, you may indeed wind up with less debt, but you will have no assets.

Our caller, Eric, told us that he has property that is worth $595,000. The bank had proposed to him that he set up a $385,000 fixed rate 30-year mortgage for which he would pay $2,300 a month on the principal and interest.

We told him that we could refinance this property, giving him a 40-year interest-only mortgage for $476,000 for which he would have to pay only $1,203 a month, a great savings. He would also come out with an additional $80,000 with the new loan.

He told us that he owed $200,000 in school payments and he would want to use the $80,000 to begin paying these down. In reality he was like the people we knew who were house rich and cash poor, only he was debt rich. Rather than pay down the debt, we suggested he take the $80,000 in usable cash and put it into some kind of savings or investment account—so that he can maintain some liquidity and hopefully earn some profit on the money.

It would appear on the surface that we make the assumption that a savings or investment account would have to earn him more than the interest rate on his loan—and that to open such an account, he'd have to take on extra risk.

What those advocating that Eric pay off his student loan often overlook is that a student loan typically has an interest that could be as low as 2%, so there is no sense in paying off a loan with such a low interest rate like that even if the interest rate were 6 or 7%. What Eric should do is take the $80,000 and put it into any kind of savings or investment account, because the interest on student loans is simple interest, while the interest on an investment or savings account, even if it's "only" between 5 and 6%, will outperform the cost of money because the interest is compounded. And, putting the money into one of these accounts provides for liquidity. If Eric uses the $80,000 to help pay off the incredibly low-cost student loan, he does not have that money available in liquid form—and he still has a remaining debt of $120,000.

So, by using the interest-only loan described above he could also take the $1,000 a month that he would be saving and pay down the debt. In the end he would wind up amortizing the debt faster than if he had pursued the original mortgage he had in mind before he contacted us.

We pointed out that he would be able to pay the overall school debt of $200,000 off faster if he spread his payments out over the next five years rather than use the $80,000 in usable cash to pay off part of the student loan. In addition, if he invested the $80,000, it would grow year after year.

At a 5 percent return on investment, the $80,000 would grow to $102,000 in five years and to $131,760 in ten years. If he paid off his debt, he would only be saving 2 percent simple interest on the $80,000.

In time, Eric, and many people like him, could develop enough usable cash to begin investing in real estate—becoming a savvy real estate investor.

You have this hidden source of cash available to you—through the equity in your home mortgages. Until you consider alternative types of mortgages, this money will continue to be unavailable to you. In your own home mortgage, you possess an asset that has hidden value. For real estate is the one asset that continues to give. In that sense, it is not like stocks or bonds that are perishable upon your selling them.

Your Mortgage Is a Wealth Creator

To succeed in this world, you've got to rid yourself of the notion that debt is bad. Once you do, you will find remarkable opportunities to create wealth. But you've got to stop thinking of a mortgage as just a way to pay off your home and begin thinking of it as a wealth creator.

People come to us having bought into the lie that banks and other financial institutions perpetrate on them—that it is better to pay off their mortgage as quickly as possible. We have had people come to our offices with Bible in hand and tell us that the Bible says it is good to be debt free.

And yes, the Bible does say that. But you cannot rely on the financial circumstances that existed 5,000 years ago for guidance on how to live today. The Bible also says that you have an obligation to take care of yourself and that means you must stop throwing money away.

When you own real estate you *can* take the cash out. You *can* put the money to work for yourself. And even after you take the cash out, you still have the asset.

Most mortgage brokers regard the whole field of real estate and mortgages as just a numbers game. But to us—and to you, too, by the time you finish this book— the name of the game is cash flow. We believe in using your mortgage not as a dead-end receptacle for your cash, but as a wealth creator that will enable you to join the emerging class of new real estate investors.

Refinancing as Insurance Against Catastrophe

The spate of hurricanes that hit southern Florida and elsewhere in the United States in 2005 reinforced the view how little advantage there is in having a paid-off home. And so it is important to tell real estate investors, new and veteran, that if your home is destroyed or severely damaged, first of all, you no longer will have the collateral; and second, you may not have the cash to complete repairs until you receive insurance—and that can take months or longer. All of this applies to homes built in tornado and earthquake country as well.

And so it is good advice for everyone to refinance periodically—they can take out some cash and put it in a bank that is different from the one with which they have a mortgage. In this way, should a natural catastrophe occur of the magnitude of hurricanes Katrina or Rita in 2005, they will have the cash to continue to make mortgage payments.

If someone living in New Orleans had been paying off a fixed-rate mortgage on a regular basis, and suddenly Katrina struck, wiping his or her house out completely, he/she would be in serious trouble financially. Had that person taken a different kind of mortgage, one in which he/she had been able to pay a smaller monthly payment and put aside cash, that cash would still have been available, even after Katrina. Often in times of natural disaster, mortgage companies forgive the loan. So there are no more mortgage payments. But the sad truth is that the person is left with no home. If the person had set cash aside, his mortgage would have been forgiven, and he would have, say, $150,000 in the bank.

Investors need to see the opportunities that exist for them to take equity out of the property. Exploiting those opportunities, they can service the debt that they have, and still get the chance for additional income.

It is important to understand that the equity that's in your real estate or investment property is really not earning any money for you, except for appreciation.

If you pay down your mortgage, you limit your ability to increase your wealth—simple as that—because the equity is now stagnant. It's just sitting there, not available to you, and not earning any money.

There is a great advantage to releasing the equity, to using it, and to leveraging it so it can be converted into cash.

Which Comes First? Finding the Mortgage or Finding the Property?

As noted in an earlier chapter, the wisest thing to do is to find a mortgage first, and only then search for the right piece of property.

To many, the idea of pinning down a mortgage first is heresy; but to us it is just common sense. The conventional thinking is that a person should find a property; and only then look around for a mortgage. But by researching mortgages first, you learn what you can afford and what the monthly payments are going to be, putting you in a much better position to go out and hunt for an ideal piece of property.

What many people do is find the property first and then see if they can afford to buy it. As a result, they enter into one grand guessing game. They chase after a mortgage, trying to fit a square peg into a round hole. If they had done the financing first, they would know in advance whether the property would work for them.

Unfortunately, most people have limited knowledge of the mortgage field so they don't know what kind of financing to look for in a real estate transaction. When they talk to a bank, they hear only about the programs that the bank is promoting. As a result, people are forced to fit the financing of their real estate into a particular mortgage program that is often not the ideal one for them.

The purchase of mortgages and the acquisition of real estate are inextricably linked.

What most people fail to appreciate is that once someone secures a mortgage for a piece of property, that property becomes more or less valuable based on the mortgage instrument that is employed. In other words, the type of financing chosen for a real estate transaction drives the real estate transaction.

By exploiting one of the newly attainable mortgage instruments that allows someone to pay back a mortgage far more slowly and to use the money that is freed up to purchase other properties or investment vehicles, the new investor can feel safe in moving forward with the purchase of real estate.

You can have a very high comfort level knowing that a mortgage has been secured that will lead to wealth creation. But you can only feel that comfort by working out the details of the mortgage first—and then finding the real estate.

Hard to Search for Property First

It's harder and harder to search for a property first. For one thing, it is difficult to find a realtor who will help someone find a piece of real estate unless they know the person has prequalified with a mortgage company.

When searching for a property, those who prequalify for a mortgage are in a better negotiating position. They know what to look for. They know whether they can afford a certain piece of property. They know the cost of money. They are unlikely to waste their time or effort—and the broker's—on real estate transactions that are not suitable or attainable.

Before looking at a property, you should look at your cash position. Normally a cash investment of 20% is required for most properties.

So if you're looking at a property, and you know that interest rates are at 6%, then you probably want to look at an interest-only mortgage rather than a 30-year term mortgage. The key is this: the lower the payment, the better the cash flow; and the better the cash flow, the better the ability to use that cash and to build up your future cash/savings account.

This is in contrast to your making payments on the principal of the mortgage. To get back that money, you either have to sell the property or refinance it, whereas if you had a lower monthly payment, you would be getting cash flow from the property.

Getting the Upper Hand

To sum up, if you know the kind of mortgage instrument that you're going to get, when you find property you have the upper hand because you now know what is the real value of the property (which is based on the net cash flow from the property). The net cash flow from the property is derived from your rental income, and the cost to you to carry the property, including your mortgage, taxes, insurance, and other expenses.

The trick is how do you continuously add real estate assets to those you already own. That is how you multiply your wealth within the shortest possible time.

Many real estate companies try to link mortgages and real estate, but they don't know how to do it successfully. The problem is that their objectives are sometimes conflicting. A real estate company that is looking to sell real estate looks at the mortgage process as simply a means to an end; the company's employees don't care what type of mortgage a person gets. All they care about is getting a mortgage so the person can close the transaction. In that way they ensure that they get their fee on that transaction. That's the way probably 90% of the real estate industry functions.

Financing First

You should always ask yourself: what is the best financing vehicle to accommodate your purchase of the real estate? The answer to this question will enable you to get the best financing and own the best real estate, as opposed to just getting whatever kind of real estate is expedient to buy at that moment.

STRATEGY #11:
LEARN AS MUCH AS YOU CAN ABOUT MORTGAGE PROGRAMS. IF YOU DON'T, YOU WILL PAY A HEAVY PRICE FOR NOT DOING YOUR RESEARCH.

If you are new to real estate and mortgages, you should learn as much as possible about the unorthodox mortgage programs. You should educate yourself about adjustable rate mortgages because those programs will be more beneficial to you in the long run.

You may not at first be interested to learn every single detail about all the newly emerging mortgage instruments. You still should do your homework to make sure you're getting the best deal. The decision you make is yours, but at least you will know the options before you decide.

Too often the financing part of a deal is not given enough thought. And yet the financing is the most important component of the real estate transaction. This is the part that will make or break you.

Obtaining Value

Real estate is just a commodity and what matters with commodities is the value. Value is driven by the method that is chosen to acquire the real estate.

Learning all about the various methods takes time and patience—and may at first seem complicated. Even after you have mastered the details of current mortgage offerings, you will have to stay on top of new and changing instruments as they become available.

N E W S M A R T
L O A N S™ :
M O R E
F L E X I B L E
M O R T G A G E
I N S T R U M E N T S

What Are New Smart Loans™?

There are a whole series of catchy names for the product that we advocate and call the New Smart Loan™.

Others call it the "Option ARM," "Cash Flow ARM," "Choice Pay, " "Flex Pay," "Personally Tailored Mortgage," the "Mortgage Stretch, " and "Advantage ARM." All amount to more or less the same mortgage product.

New Smart Loans™ are suitable for real estate investors for a number of reasons. First and foremost, they offer one of the best opportunities to leverage a mortgage with the aim of converting home equity into usable cash. They do this by providing a good deal of flexibility on monthly mortgage payments. It is the kind of flexibility that borrowers have sought for a long time but could not get until recently and this flexibility also allows the borrower to become debt free and have cash flow at the same time.

There is no need to be house rich and cash poor—not with the availability of the New Smart Loan™.

STRATEGY #12:
USE LEVERAGE TO CREATE "GOOD" DEBT.

The way to create "good" debt—the kind of debt that leads to wealth creation—is to use leverage. This may sound risky, but it is the tool that is going to bring you the profit that you are looking for. If you do not use leverage in a real estate transaction, you might as well buy a bond, because it's the leverage that increases your return on investment and increases your yield.

The New Smart Loan™ is one of the most popular of the adjustable rate mortgages (ARMs). Its main feature is that it permits the borrower—you—to choose what payments to make on the mortgage each month. Different lenders may call ARMs by different names but they share one thing in common: the interest rate can and probably will change periodically during the life of the loan.

For most ARMs, the starting or initial interest rate is frequently lower than the interest rate for a fixed rate mortgage. It is the lender's way of offering the borrower an inducement to take a risk as to whether interest rates will rise or fall.

What Is an ARM?

An adjustable rate mortgage doesn't have fixed rates, but rather has rates that change over time. It has what is called the "adjustment period" of the loan, the period between one interest change and the next. A typical adjustment period might be six months or one, three, or five years; six months and one year are the most common.

The interest rate is usually higher on longer adjustment periods—because those adjustment periods are considered more stable. For the person who wants to remain in a house for only a few years, longer-term adjustments make sense. It's then possible to exploit the lower overall interest rate on a three- to five-year ARM (as opposed to the higher-rate, fixed mortgage) and still have a high degree of stability.

Anyone who takes out an adjustable rate mortgage has to take into account that the rate (and payment) could rise at some point.

While there are all sorts of ARMs, they all base the interest rate on some index plus a margin. Lenders choose a financial index as a guide in calculating the periodic interest rate adjustment. If the index rate rises, so does the interest rate on the mortgage; and, consequently, the monthly payment increases. If the index rate decreases, both the interest rate and the monthly payment decrease.

Choosing an index can make quite a difference when the adjustment comes, as some indexes are more volatile than others. Lenders can use any of a number of indexes, but the lender must tell the borrower before signing the mortgage contract which index will be used. The most common indexes are the rates on one-, three-, and five-year U.S. Treasury securities, and the Federal Home Loan Bank Board's national or regional average mortgage rate.

The margin is an additional amount that the lender adds on to the index rate (usually from one to three points); it is constant for the life of the loan.

Interest rate caps and payment caps may apply to some loans. They ensure that abrupt and drastic increases in the index will not make monthly payments unaffordable. They are ceilings of a kind and come in two formats:

- Periodic caps, which limit the increase per adjustment period

- Overall caps, which limit the increase over the entire life of the mortgage

If you had a 2% periodic cap and a 5% overall cap on the mortgage's interest rate and the index rate climbed 3% in the first year, the interest rate would increase by only 2%. If the index rate continued to climb in subsequent years, once the interest rate reached a 5% increase it would not go any higher. Because of the reduced risk provided, however, lower periodic and overall caps can be accompanied by a higher initial interest rate.

Payment caps limit the amount the payment will increase or decrease, usually in terms of a percentage of a previous payment. Here's an example: on a $50,000, 10%, 30-year mortgage, a 2 percentage point increase in the interest rate could increase the monthly mortgage payment from $438 to $513, a 17% increase in the payment. If you had a 7.5% payment cap, however, the payment could increase to no more than $471 during the first adjustment period, a savings of $42 per month. Think of New Smart Loans™ as a set of mortgage payments, with varying monthly mortgage payments, and with varying ways to build wealth.

To appreciate all that a New Smart Loan™ offers, let's review precisely what a mortgage is and what it does:

A mortgage permits a borrower to amortize, or pay back through regular payments, the principal borrowed from a lender. Part of each regular payment is the interest; the balance of the payment is used to pay back the principal. The principal, or loan balance, decreases by the amount of the principal part of each payment. Sometimes the borrower might experience what is called negative amortization; that happens when payment is not large enough to pay all the interest due. This results in an increase in the principal due the lender.

What Is Negative Amortization?

The notion of negative amortization is very important for everyone to understand before we delve too much more deeply into smart loans. The negative amortization mortgage is one of the most popular options within the New Smart Loan™ program.

Negative amortization happens when a payment or interest rate cap keeps the actual monthly payment below the level required by the market interest rate. Because the borrower has not paid the full interest charge in the monthly payment, the unpaid interest is added to the remaining principal that is owed. This causes the outstanding balance to increase rather than decrease.

Depending on the terms of the mortgage program, the financial institution may extend the term of your contract by a year or two or calculate subsequent payments based on the new, higher, outstanding balance.

STRATEGY #13:
BE DISCIPLINED WITH YOUR NEW USABLE CASH; DON'T FRITTER IT AWAY ON BOATS AND VACATIONS.

We must make one caveat before continuing our discussion of negative amortization: the whole point of one of these New Smart Loans™ is that the borrower will have more and more usable cash on hand. But, for the borrower to become a continuing investor, he or she must exercise tough discipline on the way that usable cash is handled. If you take the cash out of the property and then go off to the track and bet on the horses, that usable cash is going to be wasted. You will be defeating the whole purpose of leveraging mortgages into wealth creators.

These mortgage instruments are not designed for people who are going to "waste" any newly found, usable cash by purchasing items that make them feel good in the short term, but prevent wealth creation over the long term. They are designed for the person who wants to take that newly found cash and put it to work, to employ that money in smart forms of wealth creation.

Four Main New Smart Loan™ Options

Although there are many different mortgage options under our New Smart Loan™ arrangement, the four main ones, varying in one way or another by the amount of monthly payments, are these:

1. The minimum-payment option: this option can result in negative amortization. As part of this option, you pay a minimum monthly start rate, the best being 1%. Depending on the lender, the start rate could be as high as 2.5% if the property is for investment purposes or second homes. The pay rate is good for the entire year.

2. The interest-only option: this option allows you to pay only the interest charged, so the principal balance neither increases nor decreases. The index is determined by the particular mortgage instrument without having to refer to the standard indexes used in the real estate industry.

   You pick the financial index that will be used and tied to the loan (plus a margin determined by the lender). Remember, the index plus the margin equals the interest rate.

3. The 15-year mortgage: this option amortizes over time (i.e., includes a payment on the principal with each monthly payment sufficient to bring the balance down to zero by the end of the mortgage's term).

4. The 30-year mortgage: this option is like the 15-year mortgage, but the monthly payment is less (and the total interest payment is greater).

The savvy real estate investor would most likely choose the New Smart Loan™ program and pay the minimum payment. That allows him/her to have more usable cash available. The money could be put to any use: a college savings fund; investing in the stock market; starting a mortgage savings account (also known as a sinking fund); or investing in other properties.

Over time, money put to these alternative uses will accumulate and compound, while utilizing the minimum monthly payment.

Generally speaking, the longer the term of the loan, the lower the minimum monthly payments will be. Many choose a mortgage with a longer term, and a lower monthly payment, to make the mortgage more affordable. Longer mortgages mean higher total interest cost, but only if the borrower retains the mortgages for the full 30 years.

Figuring Out Which New Smart Loan™ Is Right for You

Use a Total Cost Analysis to make comparisons among the four main kinds of mortgage instruments: a minimum-payment mortgage, an interest-only mortgage, and a 15- or 30-year amortization mortgage. A Total Cost Analysis makes the comparison between multiple mortgage instruments side by side. Here's an example broken down for each mortgage type so you can compare.

Let's suppose that we are taking a $200,000 mortgage on a property worth $250,000. Within the New Smart Loan™ program, here are our options:

- A minimum-payment mortgage, based on a 1.25% rate, would require a monthly payment of $667.15.
- An interest-only payment would require a monthly payment of $643.
- A 15-year payment option would mean a monthly payment of $1715.
- A 30-year payment option would cost $1314 per month.

Sometimes people incorrectly believe that choosing an interest-only payment means never having to pay off the mortgage. That is simply not true. You can pay off your mortgage—and even do it faster. Here's how:

The difference between the $667 and the $1715 monthly payments is roughly $1,000. If you take that $1,000 a month and invest it with a 5% return, at the end of five years, you will have $72,000.

If you refinance your property at the end of that first five-year period, taking 80% of its new value ($320,000, the new loan amount would be $256,000, assuming a 5% appreciation per year), you would have $56,000. That would result in a total cash return of $128,000 (the $72,000 pus $56,000 comes to $128,000). A sum of $1,000 per month equals $72,000 for the second five years.

- First five years—$1,000 per month (equals $72,000).
- End of five years—$72,000 plus $56,000 of the new loan equals $128,000.
- The sum of $128,000 at 5% equals $164,000 after the second five years.
- Adding another $1,000 per month equals $72,000 plus $164,000, or a total of $236,000 in cash at the end of ten years.

That means that over ten years, you have $236,000 working for you outside the boundaries of your mortgage obligations.

This does not mean that you have to make mortgage payments with the idea of paying off the mortgage; it simply means that you have the ability to pay it off after ten years. Had you taken a fixed rate mortgage on the $200,000, you would have had no extra money for investment purposes.

The point to be underlined here: It's advantageous to use these different kinds of mortgage programs to increase your available cash flow.

CHAPTER 6

New Smart Loans™ Give You Available Cash

The whole notion of adjustable rate mortgages (ARMs) is relatively new. Until the early 1980s, there had been no more than ten or so of these ARMs; those that did exist offered no caps and they were available for residential properties only. Back in the early 1980s, when inflation was as high as 20%, no one wanted to be tied to an adjustable rate mortgage. But when interest rates dropped—by the late 1980s—the banks came out with adjustable rate mortgages that offered annual and lifetime caps.

When the stock market collapsed in 2000, real estate began to look much more attractive as a source of investment. Properties were appreciating rapidly, and that spawned a whole new series of mortgage instruments. These new mortgages were attractive because they allowed more people to become real estate investors. People realized that one day they would want to retire, but they were hardly prepared for it: There are many things that can prevent someone from being able to borrow against the equity in their home: change in income, change in credit standing, illness, and depletion of assets, to name a few. People do not like to dwell on worst-case scenarios. But bad things happen and when they do, the person with the fixed rate mortgage is going to suffer more than the person with the minimum-payment mortgage because anyone with a fixed rate still has to pay the higher monthly payment. It is as simple as that.

STRATEGY #14:
EXPLOIT THE FLEXIBILITY OF NEW SMART LOANS™ BY VARYING YOUR MORTGAGE PAYMENTS FROM MONTH TO MONTH.

In 2003 and 2004 almost every major lender began to offer ARMs to their clients. Even banks started to offer flexible-payment mortgages, not because they were trying to encourage wealth creation (perhaps the last thing on their minds), but because they knew they were dealing with a savvier clientele. Banks might have withdrawn the ARMs at a certain point, but interest rates remained so low that these mortgages continue to be attractive.

Banks originally thought that interest rates would go down for a while, but then would go up. When banks realized that the interest rates were going to stay low, they found ARMs quite appealing. Even when interest rates were at 8.5%, banks were giving start rates of 3.95% for ARMs.

In time, interest rates on ARMs dropped lower than anyone anticipated and borrowers found that they were acquiring mortgage plans with a start rate of only 1%. The start rate covered the first five years of the plan; at the end of that period, the payment could never go higher or lower than 7.5%.

Picking a Smart Loan

The borrower's personal circumstances will determine which smart loan makes the most sense. Credit scores are the most important factor, because credit scores can determine how much a mortgage will cost. Usually, the better the credit scores, the better the pricing. Some lenders will allow a person with a much lower credit score into mortgage programs but the cost will be higher. So credit scores drive a lot of the process.

People have to qualify for one of these New Smart Loans™ just as they would for a regular mortgage. We do not advocate that people apply for a New Smart Loan™ if they cannot make the payments, based on the fully indexed rates (index plus margin). Brokers are not going to make it easier for someone to get a New Smart Loan™ than any other kind of loan. Others in the business like to give the impression that we do not require clients to qualify at a fully indexed rate—and hence we are "softening" the terms of the loan. That is just not true. To qualify for a New Smart Loan™ you'd have to qualify at the fully indexed rate. In fact, interest-only mortgage programs were designed for "A" type borrowers, not for people with low credit ratings.

Apart from credit ratings, the borrower's income is very important in determining what kind of New Smart Loan™ we recommend. To determine what kind of smart loan is best, investors should look at their objectives and needs. Most of the time investors say that their objective is to reduce their monthly payments and to be able to take more cash out of their property. This is too general a statement to be helpful. What loan you should take is determined essentially by how long you want to own the property; the type of property you are interested in; and your immediate and future cash flow needs.

One of the real advantages of the New Smart Loan™ program is the flexibility it offers in terms of money management. If your monthly income varies, you may be looking for a New Smart Loan™ to help.

We always check whether a client's income is consistent over time or whether it fluctuates. If it is consistent, then we suggest an interest-only payment mortgage for a specified period of time. If it fluctuates, then we suggest the minimum-payment option.

Never put yourself into a situation where you can't afford to make a mortgage payment.

One client told us he had been offered a 30-year fixed mortgage at 5.8% with no points. A point is equal to 1% of the loan amount. The usual guideline is that by paying two points at the closing, the borrower can receive a reduction of one quarter of a percent on the interest rate. One way to "buy down" the interest rate on a mortgage is to pay points up front. The choice is between higher initial costs/lower long-term costs or lower initial costs/higher long-term costs.

If the borrower plans to stay in a house for at least five to seven years, it could be better to pay higher initial costs (more points) in exchange for lower long-term costs (lower interest rate). But, if the borrower plans to move within two or three years, it may be wiser to minimize initial costs. All of this really has to do with how much cash the borrower has to pay with points up front verses the ability to make payments over the term of the mortgage.

To help clients decide if this was the best option, we developed a spreadsheet that showed what the person would pay monthly by taking a 30-year fixed mortgage and what he would pay by taking a minimum-payment (negative amortization) mortgage.

The minimum payments on both mortgage options that we offered him were $1,000 less than what he would have paid for the 30-year fixed mortgage he was offered at 5.8%. Thus, to have the security of a fixed rate mortgage, he would be paying over $1,000 a month.

Happily for him—he chose one of our New Smart Loan™ programs.

New investors can exploit these options for residential homes, single-family homes, condos, town houses, and for modified versions of the multifamily unit and for apartment buildings.

STRATEGY #15:
INVEST YOUR NEW "USABLE" CASH IN COMPOUND ACCOUNTS—THAT'S HOW TO BUILD WEALTH.

As has already been noted, one of the biggest advantages to investors in a real estate transaction is the use of leverage. It is the leverage that increases the return on investment and increases the yield. And it is appreciation of property values that makes it possible to do all this leveraging.

The great advantage that the New Smart Loan™ program offers is not just the opportunity to leverage, but the prospect of taking the money that is not paid into a monthly mortgage payment and simply letting it earn 5% compounded in a bank. With this usable cash increasing in size day by day, you have the advantage of watching your money grow and become more and more available for future real estate transactions.

There's no great rocket science here. The banks offer anyone the chance to earn compound interest. By taking advantage of that, the real estate investor can do much better with a New Smart Loan™ than with the more conventional fixed rate mortgages. With fixed rate mortgages there's simply no opportunity to exploit the compound interest offerings.

For example, the minimum-payment option—with negative amortization—would look something like this:

On a $262,000 property with a $210,000 mortgage, at the end of five years the mortgage would have increased to $215,000; it would have $5,000 of negative amortization.

But, by taking the money saved from making those monthly mortgage payments, the borrower winds up with $60,000 in the compound savings account, where that money has been earning 5% compounded interest.

What has happened to the property during that five-year period? It appreciated in value at 3% a year. That means the $262,000 property is now worth $304,000. So, it hardly mattered that there was $5,000 of negative amortization.

Nonetheless, if for some reason the borrower begins to feel uncomfortable creating a higher negative amortization (or deferred interest), he/she can switch over to making monthly payments on a 15-year mortgage; it's possible to go back to the minimum-payment arrangement at a later stage.

STRATEGY #16:
NEVER PAY OFF THE PRINCIPAL IN YOUR MORTGAGE.

It's very simple. As you get older, what do you need more than anything else? Cash. What in the world is a house that is paid off going to do for you? Nothing.

Recently, someone came to us. He was a hunter. In his house was a very large room and he had spent a fortune on a collection of the heads of animals that he had shot and killed—elephants, giraffes, and every conceivable animal you could think of—that were housed in this room. We called him "The Great White Hunter." He reminded us a little of Crocodile Dundee.

He had everything in creation in that room and in that house—but what he did not have was cash. He was not poor but he had no cash available to him. He might as well have been poor. He was 80 years old and he told us that he was thinking of doing a reverse mortgage. We advised him against taking a reverse mortgage because he would not get sufficient cash out of his property—and he would not have the same liquidity that he would get from other loans.

His house was worth $1.2 million.

Here is what we were able to do for him: He took out an $800,000 loan using the New Smart Loan™ program and with the help of a financial planner, he was able to take $400,000 and place it into a single premium annuity, which gave him sufficient funds to service the interest payments on the New Smart Loan™. He invested the additional $400,000 in bonds, which increased his net income and liquidity. He was particularly fortunate because he caught the bond market just as it began to really move upward.

Thanks to us, he was able to increase his liquidity and cash flow. Before, his money was as dead as all those animals were in his house. But now he was able to get the use of some cash—and do pretty well for himself.

PART III

INTEREST-
ONLY
MORTGAGES

CHAPTER 7

Interest-Only Mortgages: The Increasingly Popular Way to Free Up Usable Cash

People have been rushing to buy real estate in South Florida and elsewhere. Houses that were once priced well beyond the means of potential real estate investors have suddenly become affordable. The reason? It is the new financing method called interest-only loans.

Interest-only loans have become increasingly popular because they afford investors the chance to reduce monthly mortgage payments, while keeping that portion that would normally go toward principal either in the bank or in some kind of investment vehicle where it can continue to earn on a compounding basis.

With traditional mortgages, the monthly payment consists of an interest portion and a principal portion; over time, the amount going to the interest drops and the amount to principal increases until the loan is paid in full.

But with an interest-only mortgage, you pay only interest in the early years of the loan; later on, principal payments kick in, too, at a higher amount than with a traditional mortgage because they're paid over a shorter period of time.

These interest-only loans enable you to borrow more than you could with ordinary loans because the monthly mortgage payment does not include any funds to pay down the principal, the money that was borrowed.

Once the interest-only period is over, the payment amount grows to include payments against the principal for the rest of the term of the loan. The new payment will be larger than it would have been if it had been fully amortizing from the start so that the same principal will be paid off at the end of the loan.

A whole range of interest-only mortgages have come on the market. Some adjust every time a bank's prime lending rate changes; others come with fixed rates for three, five, seven, or ten years before they are adjusted.

To understand how these interest-only mortgages work, we have to understand the conventional mortgage first. Let's take a conventional 30-year, fixed-rate mortgage. Today, these loans charge about 5.75%. We're going to round off that figure to 6% to make it easy.

For every $100,000 you borrow, you will pay about $600 a month. That $600 payment comprises two parts. At the start, you'd pay $500 in interest, and another $100 in principal. Over time, the principal payments reduce the debt. As the debt gets smaller, the interest payments drop as well. The reason? The payments are figured each month by applying the interest rate to the remaining debt.

Since the monthly payment is always $600, a smaller portion goes to interest each additional month and a larger portion to principal. There is a snowball effect. At the start of the mortgage's final year, when only $6,400 of principal is left, just $35 a month goes to interest, $565 to principal.

Now let's look at an interest-only 30-year mortgage for the same $100,000 amount, at the same interest rate.

With the interest-only mortgage, as has been noted, there are no principal payments for the first five, seven, or ten years. The monthly payment during this period thus is only $500, compared to the $600 on the standard loan. This is a full interest payment. The payment is fixed over five years. At the end of five years, the borrowers will be paying principle and interest for the remainder of the term. What we advise clients at that stage is to come in for a "loan check-up," to see if there's new value on the property. If there is, perhaps it is time to take cash out and refinance into another five-year interest-only mortgage.

To get more specific: a conventional, 30-year loan for $150,000 at a 6% rate requires a monthly payment of $899.33. At the end of five years, the balance owed would be $139,581.54, and you would have paid the bank $53,959.80.

With the interest-only loan for the same amount at the same terms, the monthly payment would be $750. But after five years, the loan balance would still be $150,000 because you have not cut into the principal, and you would have paid the bank $45,000.

STRATEGY #17:
CHOOSE AN INTEREST-ONLY LOAN, AND HAVE THE
ABILITY TO PAY OFF YOUR MORTGAGE FASTER THAN WITH
A MORE CONVENTIONAL LOAN.

With an interest-only mortgage you can actually pay off a home faster than by relying on the more conventional loans, by making lump sum principal payments annually, quarterly, or monthly. This affords you the ability to really chip away at principal, since a regular amortizing mortgage (although comprised of principal and interest), has less going to principal over the first half term of the loan.

One concern that people have about interest-only mortgages is the fear that they will be subject to much higher interest rates after the initial five- to ten-year interest-only period ends. But with interest rates at historic lows, many variable-rate interest-only loans are capped at 12% or less over the span of the mortgage. That is a rate that many Americans need not fret about.

One argument in favor of the interest-only mortgage has been that by the time the mortgage converts into one in which the full monthly mortgage payments have to be made (usually after five to ten years), the borrower's income will have increased enough to handle the higher payments. What is statistically more likely to have happened, however, is that the borrower has moved or refinanced by the time the principle payments kick in.

There are other benefits as well. The mortgage payment is based on simple interest while any return one gets on an asset investment is based upon compounded interest. As an example: interest as simple interest on $100,000 at 5 percent over five years is $5,000 per year—or $25,000. But if you take the $100,000, at 5 percent over 5 years compounded, it is $128,335. As you can see, the compounded interest had outperformed simple interest. The money put away in a bank with compound interest is always going to do better than the money just sitting in home equity. Furthermore, with an interest-only mortgage, the investor can deduct the full payment on his/her taxes.

For young entrepreneurs whose future income may grow, interest-only mortgages allow them to buy a more expensive home now. For business executives or professionals who receive bonuses, interest-only mortgages make special sense. Borrowers make lower payments, which helps them control expenses, and then periodically apply a bonus or commission toward the mortgage principal. In most cases, they get an additional, immediate benefit of a lower interest-only payment the next month.

For families with credit-card bills, interest-only mortgages can also help. If the amount that would go toward principal on a 7% mortgage is applied instead to credit-card debt that carries 18% or higher interest, those families will come out ahead.

Interest-only mortgages will especially help the real estate investor who wants to invest in real estate because it frees up usable cash that he/she would not have had otherwise.

Suddenly, this kind of mortgage is highly popular. Almost 95% of our business involves mortgages with interest-only components.

In 2001, just 16% of all home sales in the nation were financed by interest-only mortgages. But that number jumped to 31% in the past year. In South Florida, 31.2% of home sales in the Fort Lauderdale metro area—more than double the rate of the year before—and 37.6% of home sales in the West Palm Beach/Boca Raton area were financed by these kinds of mortgages.

Interest-only mortgages are still considered unconventional and continue to only make up a small portion of the overall mortgage market; but they are becoming increasingly popular in areas where the prices of homes are high, such as California, Washington, D.C., and Chicago.

The reason for the popularity of this kind of mortgage is remarkably uncomplicated: there is simply no advantage—ever—in a real estate investor making a principal payment on a mortgage.

By committing to the interest-only mortgage, the borrower will make more money by taking the amount that would have been used to pay down the loan principal and investing it.

The interest-only vehicle benefits those individuals who understand the time-use of money and wish to keep their money working for them. This kind of mortgage is an excellent vehicle for anyone who wants to utilize a mortgage for the purpose of wealth accumulation. The greatest beneficiaries of interest-only loans are going to be those with unusual income cycles. Those who expect to be earning more money a few years into their mortgage will also benefit.

And, finally those who want to invest the money that was saved by not paying the principal in some kind of investment other than home equity. Typically, these latter people are our new real estate pros.

STRATEGY #18:
IF YOU PLAN TO LIVE IN YOUR HOME FOR ONLY A BRIEF AMOUNT OF TIME OR LONGER, CHOOSE AN INTEREST-ONLY MORTGAGE.

Interest-only mortgages are for people who plan to live in their homes for a short period of time. However, most important, these mortgages are for people who can afford the entire monthly mortgage payment. That is crucial. Otherwise, the whole effort to divert a portion of the monthly payment into investment vehicles will not work.

The interest-only program is not designed for investors who cannot make a full principal and interest payment, but for people who want to keep more of their earning dollars in their pocket or in another investment, thereby earning compound interest on their money.

That is why we call interest-only mortgages a cash management tool.

Historically, interest-only mortgages were popular prior to the Great Depression in the United States, in the 1920s and early 1930s. They were sold almost exclusively to wealthy people who wanted to free up funds for other investments.

The interest-only mortgages of the 1920s were interest-only for the entire life of the loan, typically five to ten years. What this meant was that the loan balance was the same at maturity as at the onset of the loan. Borrowers still in their homes when the loan matured would refinance.

Nothing bad came of this system of mortgage payments as long as the homes retained their value. But the real estate market did nosedive during the Depression, pushing many interest-only loans into a state of foreclosure. Viewing interest-only mortgages as stigmatized, lenders quickly switched over to fully amortizing loans, the standard mortgage loan since then.

More recently, mortgage specialists have tried to bring this highly sophisticated mortgage product to the middle market. It is considered highly sophisticated for this reason: interest-only mortgages permit borrowers to pay initially a lower monthly payment. Since, however, they are not obligated to pay against the principal, the build-up of equity is delayed. Because of this delay in building equity, these mortgages are not for everyone. Not everyone is willing to forego building up equity in a home by paying down principal.

Interest-only mortgages made a comeback once such large wholesale lenders as Fannie Mae started to offer the program. Fannie Mae started to purchase interest-only mortgages in 2001. That year, the government-sponsored enterprise bought $1.2 billion in interest-only vehicles on the secondary market. It called the mortgages "Interest First" vehicles. To qualify, the product had to be a fixed-rate interest-only mortgage with the borrower paying only the interest, tax, and insurance each month for the first 15 years of the loan. In the 16th year, the payment would grow to fully amortize the loan over the remaining 15 years of the mortgage term.

The new kinds of interest-only mortgages differ from the earlier ones of the 1920s in two distinct ways.

First, they are not interest-only for the entire term of the mortgage—only for the first five or, more typically, ten years. With the end of the five- or ten-year period, the monthly mortgage payment is hiked to the fully amortized level. In other words, once past the fixed period, these loans adjust to the fully indexed rate of the index plus the margin; the loans can adjust monthly. The mortgage essentially converts to a standard, amortizing mortgage either on an adjustable- or a fixed-rate basis.

For this reason, the more recent versions of interest-only loans seemed less risky than their counterparts from the 1920s. In fact, they are not. They are considered more risky. And here's why:

There is risk in any investment vehicle. Many people are under the misguided impression that real estate values will continue to appreciate indefinitely and consistently year in and year out. Yet real estate values are like any commodity that runs through cycles of ups and downs. Some of this has happened of late in our own real estate market in southern Florida, where people are paying X amount of dollars on a property but are unable to sell the property for more than they paid for it. It's becoming more of a buyers' market for particular product types: condominium units, single-family homes, and homes in certain price ranges or certain locations.

If you keep equity in a property there is risk, because the equity can decline if the market declines. However, if you refinance the property and take the cash out of that property, you do not come under pressure to return any of the borrowed money. As long as you make the monthly mortgage payment, the bank will not say, "Your property is worth less, so you have to give back some of the money." If a stock declines in value, however, and you have outstanding loans on that stock, you would have to pay back the money (this is known as a "margin call".)

The reason?

It turns out that limiting the interest-only period to ten years has little significance because a relatively small number of borrowers in current times keep their mortgage for that amount of time. Most are going to refinance or sell their homes while they are still in the interest-only period.

At the end of the interest-only period, the borrower can go back and refinance the mortgage, and take the five-year term all over again and possibly take some cash out of the equity.

The principal balance does not go down, but the borrower's

payments remain under control. He or she is still making a full interest payment so that is taken care of.

In the 1920s version of interest-only mortgages there was no strategy to establish a mortgage savings account (known as a sinking fund). That's why the amortized mortgage was invented: so that the principal would be paid down over time. With today's new mortgages, however, the interest rates are capped; therefore you can manage the risk better and can establish your own mortgage savings account. This gives you the choice of making those mortgage payments, applying the amount to your outstanding principle; or using it to build added wealth.

Make no mistake about it: the risk attached to ARMs is high because borrowers have exposed themselves to rising mortgage rates when market rates increase. By adding an interest-only component, the borrower only adds to the risk because when the ARM rates get adjusted at some point in the future, the new monthly mortgage payment is figured—using the original loan amount, in contrast with the smaller amount that is the balance on a fully amortizing ARM.

One can use by way of example an ARM with an interest-only payment option lasting ten years with an initial rate of 4% that resets twice a year. Worst-case scenario: the rate grows by 2% every six months, reaching a maximum of 10% by month 19.

The interest-only payment in that nineteenth month would be 150% higher than the initial payment. The fully amortizing payment, by comparison, would be "only" 82% higher.

Significantly, it is the joining of the interest-only product to adjustable-rate mortgages that have made interest-only mortgages so popular today.

Once interest-only loans were linked to ARMs, it opened the door to a whole variety of merchandising promotions that, quite frankly, were misdirected. In particular, they were promoted as new kinds of mortgages, featuring lower rates than standard fixed rate mortgages.

The truth was that the rates on interest-only loans were lower because the loans that were being touted were ARMs, not because they contained the interest-only option. It is only fair to say that, because the interest-only option increases the risk of default, the interest-only option added to any given type of mortgage increases its rate.

The Concerns Over
Interest-Only Mortgages

Though interest-only mortgages have become the mortgage vehicle of choice, it seems prudent to go over some of the potential concerns. We want you to go into these mortgages with knowledge and understanding.

Some have worried that these mortgages encourage people to take the lower payments so that they can qualify for larger mortgages, enabling them to purchase more expensive property that in reality they may not be able to afford.

Others have expressed concern that these interest-only mortgages do not permit borrowers to build equity; and as a consequence, should real estate prices drop, borrowers could wind up obligated to pay more than their homes are worth in later years.

Another concern has to do with the prospect that the index used to which the interest-only mortgage is attached could become volatile. In that case, monthly mortgage payments could begin to fluctuate more rapidly than other instruments, which would look more stable by comparison.

If interest-only mortgages come with subprime rates (the rate that a borrower with credit problems qualifies for), the margins might be higher. So that if the index moves only a bit, the size of the monthly mortgage payment could grow larger than planned for.

Needless to say, all of the above underline why it is so important to turn to a mortgage professional who can explain all of these various possibilities. The real estate investor must have some sense of how the index moves; of what constitutes the fully indexed rate; and, it goes without saying, of the length of the terms for the interest-only payment period.

It is also wise for investors to understand the degree to which they are operating in the expectation that (a) their income will increase during the time of the interest-only loan and (b) their house or houses will appreciate in value. What if these two things do not occur?

The unfortunate example is given of the person who has purchased a home for $100,000 and paid an interest-only mortgage for ten years. He has a mortgage of $80,000.

The ten years pass, the person still owes $80,000 on the house. But now that person wants to sell the house for $100,000 because he had 20% equity in the house. If property prices appreciated at only 3% a year, the property would be worth $134,935. But what happens if there is zero appreciation, or worst of all, if there is depreciation? That would leave the borrower of an interest-only mortgage owing more than the house is worth. And on occasion, this does happen.

Most lenders, however, do not concern themselves with interest-only mortgages going "under water." Home prices historically have appreciated 6% a year and that large appreciation makes such risk seem low.

Most lenders require borrowers to qualify at the fully indexed rate, including amortization, demonstrating to the lender that the borrower has the financial wherewithal to make a full payment, The banks want to make sure that, if interest rates move, the person holding the interest-only mortgage will still be able to make all monthly payments.

The key here is that interest-only mortgages work *if* the borrower is disciplined and understands both the risks and benefits associated with interest-only mortgages. We know why these mortgages are attractive—they offer a much smaller monthly mortgage payment. But they carry a risk, and we want everyone to factor in that risk before deciding on the kind of mortgage product to take. The whole premise of an interest-only mortgage is that the borrower is not going to use the money saved to go off on a winter vacation or to purchase a better car.

One young man called into our television program wanting advice on how to allocate the funds he had. At the time he called us, he was in graduate school studying to become an engineer. He was making $65,000 a year. He was renting his home and he wanted to buy his own place. He planned to graduate from grad school in two years. He assumed that his income would go up 25% by then.

His questions to us were practical: Should he buy a home now? Or should he put the money that he was able to save in a 401K, because the stock market might outperform the real estate market over the next decade? He had been putting $800 a month into a 401K.

We told him that if he could get into the right mortgage program—and there were many of them, some affording the lowest possible monthly payments—he should buy a home today, using the most amount of leverage that he could, and that he should continue to invest in his 401K.

By blending these types of disciplines, we told him, he could have his cake and eat it too. He was paying rent, but the rent was going to the benefit of someone else, someone who was paying down a mortgage or putting that cash flow into his or her own pocket.

He had no reason to wait, we said, and we asked what he thought he would be able to come up with as a down payment. "Thirty thousand dollars," he said.

We made our calculations on the basis of his purchasing a property worth $300,000. He could obtain a mortgage on a loan to value of 80%, getting a mortgage of $240,000. Using one of our New Smart Loans™ at a pay rate of 1%, he would only have to pay $771 a month. He could then get a line of credit from his bank on the $30,000 equity, which would cost him $180 a month.

So, adding $771 and $180, he would be paying $951 per month as his mortgage. Since he is in a 30% tax bracket, $285 of that $951 amount represents tax savings.

Let's say the taxes on his new property come to $5,000, or $400 a month. He would have to pay $951 plus $400, or $1,351 a month, which represents $947 net after tax savings. He is now paying $800 a month in rent. His net dollars are $949; thus he is paying $147 more, but he would own his own real estate.

People always ask how they can get the money earlier than ten or fifteen years in these mortgage savings accounts. The happy answer is that they can access their account after twelve months and take out 10% of what they invested on a regular basis. After five years they have all sorts of options, one of which is to take out all the money accumulated over that period of time.

People ask us about the interest-only mortgages and what they can do to improve their net worth. These people are put in touch with financial planners who explain how they can accumulate wealth using an interest-only mortgage.

Within that mortgage savings account there are various investment strategies to pursue. Some of the investment vehicles that generate money for these accounts come guaranteed and some do not. For all the money that someone is investing, in addition to those guarantees, we need to ensure that money is growing at the proper rate.

It is fascinating how much misinformation is disseminated by the media and also by people who are supposed to know, namely some of the people in the Federal Reserve Bank.

They have concerns about people taking money or buying property using interest-only mortgages and then finding that at the end of a five-year period these interest rates are going to be untenable, leading people to lose their properties. That shows a true lack of understanding of the way many of these mortgages work. But it also shows there is no forward thinking; there is no thinking about how borrowers can benefit from interest-only programs.

Look at the numbers at the end of five, ten, and fifteen years. The concepts are fine but it's the numbers that truly show the benefits of these programs.

Many people say that if they're able to go into a 15-year mortgage, after which their house will be paid off, they will truly be happy. What they don't understand is that the 15-year mortgage is better designed for the benefit of the bank because the bank is taking that principal payment and lending it to someone else.

There's a better way to use that money for your—and not the bank's—benefit. One option is to put the money into a mortgage savings account. This is where you put the money that didn't go into the mortgage payment into your family's bank account.

Within 15 years you will have enough equity and money in a mortgage savings account to pay off the loan. But we advise against paying it off at all. There's just no reason to.

This kind of investing requires discipline: you have to have a plan, and you have to follow through with that plan. There are some things you can build into the plan that make it easier to be disciplined. For example, you can automatically transfer money into a mortgage savings account. In this way, the borrower does not have to perform the more burdensome chore of writing a check every month.

Take the example of an investor with a property that is worth $400,000. Let us look at different mortgage programs for a mortgage of $320,000. Among these programs is one with a minimum payment and a 1% pay rate; another, an interest-only mortgage, with an interest rate of 6.17%. Then there is a 40-year amortization mortgage and a 15-year one.

The difference in payment is really what is so dramatic.

The actual interest rate is about 5.5% and the Annual Percentage Rate (APR) is about 5.86%. The APR is an interest rate that is commonly used to compare loan programs from different lenders. The Federal Truth in Lending Act requires mortgage companies to disclose the APR, which measures the true cost of a loan, when they advertise a rate.

But the pay rate on the minimum-interest mortgage is only 1%, which on $320,000 is $809 a month.

With the 15-year mortgage, the monthly payment comes to $2,600 a month. What people like about this kind of mortgage is that after 15 years, making a $2,600 monthly payment, they will have paid off their mortgage. True, they will have paid off the mortgage, but what do they have left in terms of liquid assets (usable cash)? Nothing.

If you keep that $320,000 instead of giving it back to the bank, you will have usable cash. If you do not pay off the mortgage through a fixed rate program, you will accumulate wealth much faster (oh, how money grows and grows when it's earning compound interest!)—and you will still have the property. In addition, of course, you will have enough cash in the mortgage savings account to pay off that note at any time.

But what do the banks do? They put clients in a mortgage that really benefits somebody else because they really don't believe that people have enough intelligence, enough discipline, in order to save their own money and put it into a separate account.

At the end of 15 years, if the person wants to get that money back, he or she has to go back to the bank and refinance the property.

To go back to the numbers: The minimum payment of $809 can increase slightly, by 7.5% of the $809 over the first five years.

That comes to $60. If we had $1,800 of savings between the $2,600 and the $809, you actually have $1,890 because every time you make an investment into a mortgage savings account, the payments get increased automatically by 5%; that's free money—every single time you make a deposit. At the end of five years, you will have $122,400 ($108,400 that you have deposited, and $14,000 in interest) in this account.

Calculations will show that this $400,000 property, assuming a 7% yearly appreciation, at the end of five years will be worth $561,000.

Now in the case of the $320,000 mortgage, it actually increased because you are deferring interest; so it went from $320,000 to $347,000. This is the fear that everyone talks about. They say that at the end of that period the mortgage is going to increase, Let's say yes it does: now it's $347,000.

You have $214,000 of equity as opposed to the roughly $240,000 you would have had if you were paying down the principal.

If you use this interest-only program and you make no principal payments but deposit the difference in the mortgage savings account, at the end of 14.8 years, you would have sufficient money to pay off your mortgage—and you would wind up with an additional $203,000 in cash in the bank. The earlier you can start all this, the better off you are going to be, so be sure to take advantage of the compounding of your money in a mortgage savings account without delay.

There's a need for better education about these mortgages and about what to do with the money. The conventional thinking is that once you have this money, you're going to spend it and waste it.

Is there a risk of that? Absolutely.

But it doesn't mean that people shouldn't be given that opportunity to take advantage of these programs. It's not the responsibility of the government—of Big Brother—to tell you how to manage your money.

NEGATIVE
AMORTIZATION
LOANS

CHAPTER 9

Negative Amortization: A Mouthful of a Phrase, a Generator of Quick Cash

If interest-only mortgages were meant to be an inducement to the real estate investor to divert hard-earned cash into useful endeavors, the negative amortization mortgages are an even greater inducement.

Within the New Smart Loan™ program, by far the most popular is the minimum-payment option. "Minimum payment" is another term for negative amortization.

Amortization is the gradual repayment of a mortgage loan, both principal and interest, in installments. Amortization allows for monthly payments that are big enough to pay the interest and reduce the principal on a mortgage.

Negative amortization happens when the monthly payments do not cover all of the interest cost. The interest cost that is not covered is added to the unpaid principal balance. This means that even after making monthly payments, you could owe more than ou did at the start of the loan. Negative amortization can occur when an ARM has a payment cap that results in monthly payments not high enough to cover the interest due.

Don't be fooled by the word "negative" in negative amortization. It does not necessarily mean the whole concept is something to be avoided. Such mortgages have a lot to offer.

Before addressing the question of how a negative amortization mortgage works, consider how a positively amortizing loan functions.

As noted earlier, the conventional mortgage loan requires of the borrower monthly payments of principal and interest; these, over the term of the loan, lead to the principal amount being paid off. The process of paying off that loan is called amortization. The portion of each monthly payment that goes toward principal and interest changes with each payment made. In the early years of the loan, most of the monthly payment goes toward the interest, but at some point in the middle of the term the proportion changes so that, in the end, most of the payment goes toward the principal.

Payments also may be made that include, in addition to principal and interest, an extra amount that is applied to the principal and thus accelerates the reduction of the loan balance.

The option we are discussing in this chapter has artificially low payments that the lender will accept, but these payments do not pay for all of the interest due, nor do they pay for any of the principal. The remaining interest that was due for the month but not paid is added to the principal balance of the loan, causing the balance to increase and negative amortization to occur.

With numerous payment options from which to choose, there is much flexibility for the borrower. Especially appreciating this flexibility are borrowers whose income varies or whose financial situation is complicated.

Usually, banks and other financial institutions are prepared to accept negative amortization on the condition that the original principal does not grow beyond a predetermined ceiling, such as 110–125% of the original loan amount.

STRATEGY #19:
TO PURCHASE A LARGER HOME WITH A LOWER MONTHLY MORTGAGE PAYMENT, CHOOSE A NEGATIVE AMORTIZATION MORTGAGE.

A negative amortization mortgage is a mortgage that permits the borrower to defer some of the interest that is due each month to later in the life of the mortgage. The great advantage is that someone can purchase a larger home with a lower initial monthly mortgage payment. However, the borrower is required to qualify at the fully indexed rate based on a 30-year amortization. In effect, the borrower is being given a minimum-payment rate at the start of the loan and a gradual increase of payment over the next five to ten years, in contrast to having a fixed rate for the entire loan.

Specifically, negative amortization constitutes the unpaid interest that is added to the mortgage principal in a loan in which the principal balance rises rather than falls because the mortgage payments do not cover the full amount of interest due.

Adjustable-rate mortgages typically have this feature because the "amortizing interest rate" is higher than the required "payment rate." During times when interest rates are low, the amortizing rate can be lower than the payment rate, causing "positive amortization" or the reduction of principal. Recently, these types of loans have been tied to various indexes: the most popular are the 12-Month Treasury Average Index; the Cost of Funds Index, known as COFI; and the one-month London Interbank Offered Rates (LIBOR) Rate.

There is a distinct advantage to investors in taking out negative amortization mortgages: these mortgages routinely permit a borrower to potentially increase his or her cash flow and reduce monthly payments. This means that the investor can manage the risks of investment better.

STRATEGY #20:
IF YOU KNOW THAT YOUR INCOME WILL INCREASE DRAMATICALLY IN THE NEAR FUTURE, CHOOSE THE "NEGAM" MORTGAGE OPTION.

If your income will increase dramatically in the near future, this mortgage also will allow you to make higher payments to "cover the interest rate" and reduce the principal once your income goes up.

There is every reason to think favorably of "negam" mortgages, as they are called. It is as if you've been given a favorable credit line that permitted investing in your dream home. The one thing that you must make sure of is that the mortgage contains some form of annual interest rate "cap" as well as a ceiling on the interest rate that can be charged over the life of the loan.

Negative amortization mortgages are the most talked about and most interesting of the new mortgage instruments available to you. The reason is simple: By paying no principal payments and deferring interest payments, you make lower monthly payments. As long as you place the cash that would have gone into the higher monthly payments into your own mortgage savings account, you become your own bank. Instead of making principal payments to the bank, you make payments only to yourself, into your own mortgage savings account.

A mortgage savings account can be all sorts of things: it could be a transaction, or an insurance policy, or a certificate of deposit, or a regular savings account. It is, in all these cases, the place where a borrower puts his or her excess cash.

The negative amortization mortgage, essentially a deferred-interest loan, is the most misunderstood mortgage program for no other reason than it has so many options. Its advantage lies in its flexibility, i.e., the borrower gets to choose between making the full loan payment, the minimum payment, or any amount in between.

There are many people whose incomes vary throughout the course of a year. Some people get paid commissions or bonuses. Some people get paid on an irregular basis with many months of not being paid in between. Budding real estate pros fall into this latter category. They cannot possibly know when or how often or in what quantities they will be paid over a 12-month period. The "negam" mortgage is the perfect solution for such people.

If your income varies throughout the year, you can make a lower payment during the more difficult times, and then make higher payments when there is readily available cash.

In these negam situations, you are "deferring" some of the interest, because if your interest-only payment is $1,000 a month but you are paying an $800 minimum payment, you have a spread or difference between interest-only payment and that minimum payment of $200. That difference is referred to as deferred interest, and it gets added to the principal every month.

Hence, you have negative amortization: instead of the mortgage amortizing positively where the principal is dropping, the principal or the amount of the loan is going up because the minimum payment is lower than the interest you are in fact being charged.

It is, of course, quite possible to avoid negam simply by paying the interest-only payment. Then there is no difference if the interest rate moves up or down: the person always pays the maximum amount of interest.

A negative amortization mortgage can be a very good thing; but you must keep in mind that, by permitting a super-low monthly mortgage payment, a negam loan increases your overall debt.

Problems arise when lenders advertise negam programs. They sometimes make erroneous statements about what such programs are. For instance, one mortgage company's advertisement touted a negam program by calling it an "interest-only" payment, and then declaring, "Our interest-only mortgage allows you to trim your mortgage."

That, of course, is nonsense. We are talking about a mortgage program that does not curtail principal. It cannot "trim" a mortgage. It can lower your monthly payment, but the balance on the loan does not change.

There are other ways in which you can get confused over the way a negative amortization loan works:

The minimum payment on negam mortgages is frequently based on some predetermined calculation, perhaps a 30-year amortization with an interest rate of 1%. So, on a $300,000 loan, the minimum monthly mortgage payment would be $965. This 1% should be referred to as the "payment rate" because it most likely is not the true interest rate of the loan.

This mortgage carries an adjustable rate linked to a popular index, the Monthly Treasury Average, which at present yields 2%. The loan carries a margin that usually ranges between 2.5% and 3.5% over the index, depending on the particulars of the loan— but it can get as high as 5.5%.

To avoid negative amortization, you would have to make a payment that is sufficient to cover the interest charged at 4.5%. This interest-only payment would come to $1,125. But your minimum payment is $965. If you make the minimum payment, the difference is added to the mortgage balance, increasing the loan to $300,160.

Many borrowers confuse the "payment rate" with the actual interest rate. This is hardly surprising, given that radio and newspaper advertising sometimes promise "rates as low as 1%." They should not be making such promises.

Here's another example of how a negative amortization, or deferred-interest, mortgage works. It permits a minimum monthly payment that is less than the interest owed for that month. So instead of reducing your balance every month, the unpaid interest for that month is added to the principal balance. What this means is that the mortgage balance increases as time goes on.

Let's say that you take an interest-only adjustable rate mortgage that carries an 8% interest rate.

If the loan were for $200,000 you would have to pay a monthly interest of $1,333 (8% times $200,000 divided by 12 months). If you pay $1,333 each month, the $200,000 balance does not change.

STRATEGY #21:
SELECT A NEGAM MORTGAGE IF YOU WANT TO INCREASE YOUR CASH FLOW IN THE SHORT RUN.

Though people have warned investors against using negam mortgages, savvy new real estate pros realize the advantages—and are profiting from these mortgages. Their greatest reason for relying on these mortgages is the increased cash flow they provide and the opportunity to reduce their debt-to-income ratios. Cash, as we cannot say often enough, is king.

You know that getting your hands on money today is far better than having money available tomorrow. The idea is to stop giving money to the bank and give it to yourself instead. Isn't it better to have cash now than somewhere down the road? Of course it is. That's why you should go with the negam mortgage program.

If you have the ability to make a larger mortgage payment, but have the option of paying a smaller one, we say you should make the smaller mortgage payment to the bank, and put the rest of the money aside. In that way, you are paying yourself, not the bank.

The best advice is for new real estate investors to take the money that they save and invest it in any one of a variety of vehicles that, at the worst, will pay a 4% rate of return. At least the borrower is earning something, whereas if he or she gave it to the banks, it would go into what could be called a dead equity account.

Moving through the numbers one last time: If a person has $200,000 in equity in his or her home, how much in interest does it earn every year?

Zero.

That is not a good rate of return. It's the not the rate of return that a real estate pro is looking for on an investment.

By taking out a negam loan, we are ensuring that our money works for us, not for the bank. We can invest the money that we are saving by putting it into a monthly mortgage savings account; and we can invest that money and earn a compound rate of return.

Let's look at what we call the "power of compounding":

With a 30-year $200,000 negam mortgage, if you take the $700 that you would have paid into a monthly mortgage payment and deposit it in a compound account that gives a 4 percent rate of return, you will have accumulated $204,000 at the end of 17 years.

What could you do with that money?

Well, one thing would be to pay off the $200,000 mortgage—13 years ahead of when it would have been paid off using a conventional mortgage. And there would still be $4,000 in cash left over.

More on Negam Mortgages—and Why They Are Gaining More and More Adherents

The question on everyone's mind at this point is: How could I possibly pay off my mortgage quicker without affecting my cash flow?

It's really very simple.

Most people think there are only two easy ways to pay off a mortgage quicker—by inheriting money or winning the lottery. But these are not things you can factor into your financial planning easily.

You could, of course, make extra payments on the mortgage, but if what we've written on these pages has sunk in at all, you know we are dead set against making extra payments.

Many people come into our office and say: "I want to pay off my mortgage faster."

We ask them why. Sometimes the person tells us: pride of ownership. Sometimes they tell us they want to be debt free; or, to get a better cash flow.

"Great answer," we say in reply, but we then note, "We can show you how to accomplish that and never make a principal payment. Are you interested?"

We then run through a scenario for them, what we call a Total Cost Analysis:

Let's say that you have a property that is valued at $262,500. You have taken out a negam loan of $210,000. So you will not make any principal payments, but will pay primarily interest-only payments. Points are 1%; the index is 2.17%; the margin is 2.6%; and the life cap is 9.95%.

The monthly mortgage payment on the $210,000 loan is $675.

If we compare that to a 30-year fixed rate mortgage, which would have a rate of 5.75%, the monthly mortgage payment would come to $1,226. Hence, there is a spread in payment between $675 and $1,226 of $551.

The banks are going to be more than happy to take the $1,226. They will clear that money in a day and keep the funds you just gave them. This is why we never see a bank lodged in a tent, only in a beautiful building. There are no poor bankers, believe me. Your goal should be to become the bank. You want to maximize your return on investment.

The negam mortgage gives you the choice of making three payments each month to pay down the $210,000 loan:

- $675 on a New Smart Loan™, or option ARM
- $1,661 on a 15-year fixed
- $1,226 on the 30-year fixed

The largest difference in the amount of monthly payments is $986.

Here's how you can become the bank. You use the $986 you have saved by taking the New Smart Loan™ or the option ARM rather than the 15-year fixed, and deposit it in a compounding mortgage savings account, earning an average return of 5%.

We discussed a question earlier: How do you repay a mortgage quicker without it affecting your cash flow?

Here's how it's done:

If you were in a 15-year fixed mortgage, you would pay $1,600 monthly. But if you took the smart loan at $675 a month and used the $985 difference wisely, you could pay off the mortgage in 12 years—three years less than if you paid it all off in the course of the 15-year fixed rate mortgage. You can then decide to pay off the mortgage in 12 years, or keep that money earning compounded interest at 5% for the next three years—an extra $34,000.

What have you become? You have become the bank. You've done what the bank does. You've just loaned your money to yourself.

You certainly don't want to give the bank the chance to lend your own money back to you.

If you have access to that $900, isn't it better in your pocket when you take into account what was said earlier?

If you had $1 million on the table, which is the equivalent to having no mortgage on your property, if you had that equity sitting in your property and you could not convert that into cash, what's going to happen to you? You are going to starve to death. It's plain and simple.

And whether you believe it or not, there are many people out there that are doing the same thing. They live in a $1 million house and they are starving to death because they did not plan; because they bought into the nonsense that they have to have a debt-free property; because it makes them feel good to be free of debt.

What makes you feel *really* good is a full belly.

And don't think it isn't that basic. Go two days without eating. You're not going to think of anything else but whether you have money to buy food. That's why it's very important to convert equity to cash.

If you put money into an interest-bearing account as opposed to in a home, you can pay off a 15-year mortgage without making extra mortgage payments.

This is one reason why the negam mortgage is the best available for new real estate investors: it gives them the most flexibility and the greatest management of cash. And that is one thing that no one talks about: the management of cash. It should be discussed, widely, loudly, often, for cash is what enables us to buy commodities—those things that we feel are necessities.

If someone says, "I want to lock into a 15-year, or a 30-year mortgage" or, "I want to pay off my mortgage," what they are doing effectively is creating a void in their cash management. They are essentially making their cash position worse instead of better.

If the monthly payment on a 30-year loan is $1,200 a month while the minimum payment on a negam mortgage is half that, $600, there is nothing preventing the borrower from making the $1,200 payment. There is just no *obligation* to make the $1,200 payment. The only obligation is to make the $600 payment.

So if you are paying attention to your cash position, you will want to maximize the use of your money by setting up your own savings account with a bank, instead of giving that equity component back to the bank. You can either set up a Certificate of Deposit (CD) or make payments to a Roth IRA Account; you can buy more real estate, take out insurance policies, or buy annuities.

By making smaller mortgage payments, you are empowering yourself to use your own money in a more intelligent manner, as opposed to turning it over to the bank in principal payments. When you give it back to the bank, *it* has these options—to lend that money to someone else or—worse yet—to lend it back to you.

So, to summarize:

- Make smaller mortgage payments to attain positive cash flow.
- Establish a mortgage savings account.
- Focus on this motto: a properly structured mortgage is the cornerstone of a wealth creation strategy.

The most important thing you need for financing property is leverage. The mortgage is the key to that. And to have a properly structured mortgage, you need a payment strategy. To develop that strategy, you must ask yourself certain questions:

- How am I going to pay for a mortgage?
- Am I going to pay quickly and then make money while locking all my equity into the property, making it dead equity?
- Do I want to pay interest only?
- Do I want to keep most of the equity in the property?
- Or do I want to pay into a negam mortgage? Do I feel comfortable with such a mortgage?

Let's talk about the positive cash flow that comes from a negam mortgage.

Here are the great advantages of this type of mortgage: The money comes to you. You pay the bank. But you pay the bank very little because you are involved in either a negam mortgage or an interest-only one.

Having a positive cash flow gives you a couple of great benefits: you pay less money to the bank, which means lower debt-to-income ratios, which in turn means you can purchase more investment property.

What are the advantages of a negam loan over an interest-only loan?

The negam option enables you to manage the best possible mortgage payment or the lowest possible mortgage payment because you are making what is considered a minimum payment. By using the negam mortgage instrument you would be able to pay off your mortgage in 12 years as opposed to 15 years.

So in other words you would actually have more money at the end of that period of time than you would if you were to use a conventional mortgage.

Can the new investor use a New Smart Loan™ program (including the negam option) to do real estate transactions?

The answer is yes in many instances, primarily for residential homes: single-family homes, condos, and town houses. The program can also be used on a modified version of the multifamily home and for apartment buildings.

T H E   N E W   R E A L   E S T A T E   I N S T R U M E N T S

CHAPTER 11

Gaining a Tax Advantage: Performing Tenants in Common Real Estate Transactions

Tenants in Common and 1031 Exchanges are the fastest growing real estate transactions occurring in commercial real estate. Tenants in Common (TIC) transactions have become more prevalent in the last two or three years: more and more people are choosing them over limited partnership or limited liability companies. They buy properties under an ownership title called tenants in common. 1031 Exchanges will be covered in the following two chapters.

Tenants in Common arrangements have become quite popular in recent days because the real estate industry has come to appreciate the great tax advantages that they offer. A TIC is a kind of joint tenancy that can be offered as a replacement property investment to 1031 exchangers. TICs have sponsors that purchase the property and apply for financing on the property. The properties are usually triple-net with A-rated tenants. TICs are at times sold as securities and sometimes as real estate.

The SEC considers TICs as securities (if not both securities and real estate). If it is considered a security, only a securities broker-dealer can sell it: investors are given special disclosures and protections.

Some TIC companies rely on legal opinions that TICs are real estate and not securities and can be sold directly by the sponsor. TICs are normally considered as a possible replacement property by investors who have managed a property (the relinquished property), but are looking for less active management in their replacement property.

A TIC transaction, also known as a Tenancy In Common investment or a Co-ownership of Real Estate (CORE), represents co-ownership of real estate by two or more investors.

The Tenants in Common arrangement is a kind of ownership in which two or more parties have an undivided interest in the property. The owners may or may not have equal shares of ownership, and there are no rights of survivorship. However, each owner retains the right to sell his or her share in the property as he or she sees fit. When two or more tenants own a property, if one owner dies, the other does not automatically take over the entire estate.

Tenants in Common arrangements enable people to have individual ownership of the property in question. We recommend that people buy real estate property using a TIC and that they especially do it through an entity known as a limited liability company. In other words, the person forms a single member LLC to purchase his/her interest as a tenant in common. The individual ownership of the LLC is viewed as a disregarded entity for tax purposes, which means that the tax benefits flow through to the individual but the individual is protected from liability using the LLC.

Most people don't understand that one big, big advantage of the TIC transaction is the ability to use a 1031 Exchange. That exchange enables someone to buy into larger projects, as a result of which they have the potential of deferring more taxes, rolling those tax deferrals into more properties over a period of time. TIC investors possess undivided interests in the property or designated interests of differing sizes.

As a TIC/CORE investor, you are on the deed and considered a direct owner of the real estate. You share "pro rata" in the income, tax benefits, and appreciation of the property.

Tenants in Common investment properties employ professional asset and on-site property management, guided by a Tenants in Common agreement, which sets forth the governance of the property and the decisions requiring a vote by the property owners.

When the person dies, the property portion is transferred to the decedent's beneficiary.

STRATEGY #22:
USE TENANTS IN COMMON AGREEMENT IN ORDER TO MAKE IT EASIER TO USE 1031 EXCHANGES AND COST SEGREGATION ANALYSES.

These arrangements enable the budding real estate pro to utilize functions like a 1031 Exchange and cost segregation analysis more effectively than such traditional ownership vehicles as limited partnerships, limited liability companies, and S corporations— because Tenants in Common are treated more as independents than they are as central management.

Since 2001, the Tenants in Common industry has grown roughly 100% every year. By 2004, some $4 billion was invested in the Tenants in Common business, up from approximately $10 million in 1994. Why have TICs become so popular?

Newly minted real estate pros are awakening to liquidity options heretofore unavailable. Rapidly growing numbers of accredited investors are turning to Tenants in Common transactions to achieve rapid liquidity and to defer capital gains on their real estate holdings.

Other benefits of these transactions include professional management while being able to achieve cash flow, tax benefits, appreciation, and debt pay-down.

Smart Loans and TICs

If two people, Joe and Randi, wanted to buy an investment property together and they're not related or married, they can use a New Smart Loan™ program to finance a TIC: they must structure the transactions as a TIC—which means they own their interest individually, not together.

The difference between a TIC and a rights of survivorship agreement is that under a right of survivorship arrangement, if Joe dies, his interest goes to Randi or vice versa. But under a TIC arrangement, Joe's interest goes to his estate and Randi's goes to her estate.

If I owned 50% of a real estate transaction and you want to buy my interest, you can't finance the half, you'd have to finance the whole transaction.

Tenants in common agreements afford a new investor a couple of advantages that will become apparent when we get into a discussion of exit strategies using a 1031 Exchange later in this chapter.

If the owner of a property with a realized profit in that property wants to utilize a 1031 Exchange, he or she has to identify another property to buy into in order to take advantage of a 1031 Exchange.

Let's say that you sell a property, realizing a profit of $300,000.

You must take the $300,000 to a qualified intermediary who holds all the money. (We define a qualified intermediary in a later chapter.) Then when you identify a new property, you can take that profit and buy into that new property and defer the gain. That is a potential tax savings of roughly $45,000 on the $300,000.

The owner of property "A" buys into property "B" for $300,000, deferring $45,000 in taxes. The buyer of property "B" can now buy into a TIC. This is important because if you have only $300,000, you may not be able to buy into another property for more than $300,000. The rule is you can buy equal or greater than the money you are putting in. So the $300,000 goes into a TIC. The transaction I just did has a minimum investment of $330,000.

We get back to the notion of exit strategy that we mentioned above.

Now you can get out of the property you're in and latch on to another property utilizing the method of 1031 Exchange. You can also use the TIC.

More and more the new real estate pro is beginning to use this very sophisticated instrument, the TIC.

STRATEGY #23:
USE TENANTS IN COMMON OPTION TO GET TAX-
SHELTERED CASH FLOW.

Once you buy into a TIC, you will have that $300,000 in the TIC during a time that is beneficial to you. By doing this you are getting tax-sheltered cash flow on the total amount. So if you sold an investment property, and made $300,000, at the end of the year you write a check to the government for $45,000. You now have at that point $300,000 minus the $45,000. You have a $255,000 investment.

In order for you to get even (back to the $300,000), what return do you need and how long will it take you? If you're looking at the future value of $300,000 and a present value of $255,000, you're looking at an interest rate of 7%.

Thus, it would take 2.33 years to get back to the $300,000. That's a lot of time just to get back to where you were originally. So when you look at an exit strategy, isn't it better to have that $300,000 working for you, even if in the future you have to pay taxes? You're now earning money on that $45,000.

However, you have the ultimate tax shelter in real estate. It's not the best solution. It's not the one you would choose all the time but it's going to happen whether you like it or not. Upon death, the basis for your property increases.

Let's say you started out in a property for which you paid $50,000—and you've been able to do these 1031 Exchanges over a period of years and now 30 or 40 years pass, and then you die.

Let's say that the $50,000 you invested is worth $1 million. The real estate is worth $1 million. Upon death the basis now goes up to $1 million if your heirs were to sell their property at that time.

The heir tax liability that you had been deferring for 30 or 40 years moving from one thing to another is now zero. You're not liable for paying taxes after you die. Taxes go to your estate.

The property that is worth $1 million goes to your heirs. Your heirs now continue to do these 1031 Exchanges until they die and now the basis goes forever higher.

One assumes at some point in the future your heirs will have to sell the property and they will have to pay the tax. The tax can no longer be deferred. Then you discuss contributing the property to a charitable remainder trust.

At that point your heirs get a deduction for the value of the property for the charity. Your heirs now become trustees of the charity; they can take a salary or an annuity. They can contribute the real estate to a church or synagogue, for example, and the charity pays an annuity for the rest of their lives.

This is tax-deferred heaven.

No vehicle in this country is a better vehicle than real estate. When you start to use these strategies with a financial planner it only gets better. That is because over a period of time the tax laws have favored real estate over all other instrument vehicles. What is the reason for this? Most politicians own real estate. It's as simple as that.

CHAPTER 12

1031 Exchanges: Another Great Vehicle to Defer Paying Taxes

We will focus this chapter and later chapters on various real estate strategies that we use.

Not a lot of people know about a great real estate investment strategy known as the 1031 Exchange. Newer real estate investors have begun to learn about them only recently, but they have long been a favorite tax-deferral tool for owners.

The 1031 Exchange allows you to defer paying capital gains when you sell one property for another. It allows you—if you own a piece of property that was for investment purposes or used in a trade or business—to exchange that property for another property of like kind. And if you follow the rules, you will use a qualified intermediary that acts as an independent third party to ensure safe harbor.

Like Kind Exchanges involve business or investment property that is exchanged for like kind property. Like-kind exchanges must not involve constructive receipt of cash for the property relinquished. So the use of a qualified intermediary can facilitate the exchange using escrow accounts. The particular intermediary promises to return the proceeds of the exchange to the transferor of the property.

If you follow all the rules governing 1031 transactions, you won't have to pay any taxes. A 1031 thus is a tax-deferral technique.

The 1031 strategy applies only to investment properties, not personal residences. For personal residences you would use section 121 of the tax code, and this is not a deferral but a total exclusion of the tax up to $500,000 of the gain (if you are a married couple) or $250,000 of the gain (if you are single). By knowing both of these strategies you can find the way that will benefit the taxpayer the most. If you had a personal residence and lived in it for two of the five years prior to its sale, you could sell it under section 121 and exclude up to $500,000 of the gain; if the gain is to be larger you may want to consider changing use and using section 1031.

Here's an example: Let's say I own an investment property that is a condo and I had done a 1031 before I bought it. I deferred $100,000 in tax in that condo because I had done a 1031 Exchange into it. Now let's say that I hold the condo as an investment property for two years, getting rent from it; but I then decide to move into it and make it personal property.

If I live in it for three years (not just two, because it was purchased through a 1031 Exchange) as my personal property, and the total exclusion is $500,000 (if a married couple) or $250,000 (if a single person), I can exclude the entire $500,000 or $250,000 under section 121 of the IRS Code.

But after three years, if the property appreciates to $1 million, I might want to consider changing the use back to investment property, rent it out for a year, and sell it under section 1031.

Notice that I can't reap the tax advantages by treating the property both as an investment property and as personal property.

STRATEGY #24:
USE A 1031 EXCHANGE AND AVOID PAYING CAPITAL
GAINS WHEN SELLING PROPERTIES.

The idea of 1031 Exchanges has been around since 1921 and it's amazing that more people don't know about it. Very few in the past took advantage of this type of tax advantage, although it was certainly available. The idea is named after the section of the United States tax code, section 1031.

The purpose of the section originally was to keep investment in America. Hence, the government started 1031 Exchanges. What the government was saying was this: if you reinvest in more real estate, we will defer the capital tax gains.

The whole topic of 1031 Exchanges used to be a lot more complicated. Judicial decisions in the late 1970s and early 1980s, the so-called *Starker* cases, simplified matters. These cases led the IRS to create new rules in 1991 that govern the way 1031 Exchanges must be carried out.

The *Starker* decisions set up rules for a delayed exchange. These rules permit a taxpayer to reinvest proceeds from the sale of property held for investment or business purposes into another investment or business property and defer all the capital gains that normally would have been paid.

The result has been an explosion in the use of 1031s as an investment and tax-deferral vehicle, particularly in certain sections of the United States.

The 1979 *Starker* ruling allowed property used in a trade or business or held for investment to be exchanged purely for like-kind property, which would be used in a trade or business or held for investment, tax-free.

What is meant by "like-kind property"? The properties involved in a tax-deferred exchange must be similar in nature or characteristics. Like-kind real estate property is basically any real estate that isn't your personal residence or a second home.

A deferred exchange allows the taxpayer to relinquish property currently and receive like-kind replacement property in the future. However, in view of the administrative nightmare that *Starker* created, and the potential for abuse of the tax system through the deferred exchange, five years after *Starker* (1984) Congress limited the scope of that decision by enacting Section 1031(a)(3), a provision of the tax code that allowed deferred exchanges to occur only within a specific time frame. Here is what the relevant section says:

> For purposes of this subsection, any property received by the taxpayer shall be treated as property which is not like-kind property if—
>
> (A) Such property is not identified as property to be received in the exchange on or before the day, which is 45 days
>
> (B) Such property is received after the earlier of—
>
> (i) The day which is 180 days after the date on which the taxpayer transfers the property relinquished in the exchange, or
>
> (ii) The due date (determined with regard to extension) for the transferor's return of the tax imposed by this chapter for the taxable year in which the transfer of the relinquished property occurs.

So a 1031 allows you to defer paying capital gains tax if you do it in a timely fashion. Taking advantage of this 1031 Exchange means having much more money in your hands, which in turn allows you to buy a much larger property or more properties if you wish. If you do it correctly, you may never pay taxes.

Section 1031 Exchanges of real estate have long been a favorite tax-deferral tool for owners. In these Exchanges, business or investment property is disposed of through a qualified intermediary, and the proceeds are used to purchase a replacement property of like kind. This results in a deferral of all or most of the gain that otherwise would be subject to income tax on the sold property.

The replacement property has a carryover tax basis that is generally the value of the replacement property minus the gain deferred in the exchange.

Many are using the 1031 Exchange conventionally. They have a property; they sell it, put money into a qualified intermediary, then find another property and use the money to do more property. Those are larger, commercial transactions.

Many people think of 1031 Exchanges as a gimmick, even though, as we said earlier, they date back to the 1920s. But they are not gimmicks at all. Done properly, they are the equivalent of an interest-free loan from the Internal Revenue Service.

The Pros of Doing a 1031 Exchange

There are a number of good reasons why you would want to do a 1031 Exchange.

Under Internal Revenue Code Section 1031, "Tax Deferred Exchange," you can participate in a real estate exchange and never pay taxes: "The taxpayer may avoid the taxable sale and purchase, and qualify for exchange treatment, if, prior to the sale of the old property, the taxpayer enters into an exchange agreement with a 'qualified intermediary,' who structures the exchange transaction properly to meet all of the requirements of the code and the regulations."

Basically, a 1031 Exchange provides greater proceeds for the client's next investment than if he/she used after-tax profits for reinvestment.

As long as the exchange is a "like-kind" real estate investment, the 1031 provides clear-cut advantages. Like-kind properties are defined as investments in "business land/properties that are considered to be the same type and exchanging them is therefore tax free."

You have to have special language in your contract that would say something like this: the seller and the buyer agree to cooperate to facilitate the seller to do a 1031 Exchange.

If I'm an investor I want to put in all of my contracts that I may want to do a 1031 Exchange—even if I don't want to—because it gives me an option for 45 days to decide whether I want to or not. The cost is negligible, under $500.

STRATEGY #25:
SELECT A 1031 EXCHANGE TO ACQUIRE A MORE VALUABLE PIECE OF REAL ESTATE THAN THE ONE BEING SOLD.

One advantage of the 1031 Exchange is the ability to acquire a more valuable piece of real estate than the one being sold. This is especially useful if the investor hopes to use the proceeds from the sale of a business or investment property to purchase more of that item. This is called the "napkin rule" because the rule was originally written down on a napkin in some bar.

In a 1031 Exchange the seller of the property must be the same person as the buyer of the property. Now that can be a problem. If a husband has property in his name only and he's selling it and it's going to be a 1031 Exchange, he would have to be the buyer of the property. He couldn't buy the new property in both of his and his wife's name.

Here's an example of how this would work:

An investor sells someone else an investment property from his or her real estate portfolio for a sum of $2.5 million. Using a 1031 Exchange, the investor "exchanges" that investment property for another property of equal or greater value. The investor avoids paying the capital gains on the $2.5 million sale and is afforded the opportunity to use the tax savings to acquire a potentially more valuable property.

The Internal Revenue Service does stipulate that the "exchanged" property must be of equal or greater value than the piece sold. Also, the exchanger can't collect additional benefits or cash without paying capital gains taxes on this money. Still, the potential for tax savings is quite large.

Two Types of 1031s

There are two types of exchanges, a forward and a reverse. Reverse exchanges will not be discussed here because they're very expensive, very technical, and people don't like to do them. Forward exchanges are generally what is being done in the marketplace.

A forward exchange works like this:

Someone sells a property first and then buys another piece of property, to reinvest in. Now when the property is sold, the money has to go to a qualified intermediary (QI). You are not permitted to own two properties at once. You can't touch the money. If you do touch the money, it automatically disqualifies a 1031 Exchange.

The big advantage of the 1031 Exchange obviously is deferred gain. Right now capital gains are taxed at the low rate of 15%. They won't hold that way forever.

The Department of the Treasury is very lenient when it comes to the conditions it places on the properties. Its only condition is that the properties in question must be in the United States. They can be raw land or commercial or residential property.

You must buy a property that is at least equal or greater to the value of the relinquished property. If you have debt on the old property, the exact amount must go on the new property.

Don't do what some people do: sell a property and let the money from the sale sit with a QI. They then go out and find a property for the same amount of money or more. They buy it and they decide to put a bigger mortgage on the property. If you do that, the transaction is taxable.

What happens if you put your money with a QI, and then you can't find a property or you change your mind? It's a taxable event. You'll have to pay the taxes.

Partnership interests do not qualify for a 1031 Exchange. Tenants in Common do qualify, but be careful with that tool. The seller may tell you it's a TIC, but the IRS may not look at it as a TIC. It may look at it as a partnership.

The 1031 is a sophisticated and unique tax method wherein accountants can provide the necessary expertise to ensure the proper implementation of this wealth accumulation strategy.

Even early-stage real estate pros can benefit from 1031 Exchanges, and accountants can provide several important 1031 services. Favorable tax advantages, such as those provided for in 1031 Exchanges, can be a marketing vehicle that can create a window of opportunity for the accountant with vision.

In the 1970s and 1980s we have seen the infancy and growth of several lucrative specialties, including estate planning, financial planning, and pension planning.

The 1991 IRS Exchange regulations have made the 1990s "The Golden Era of the 1031 Exchange." However, despite the age of the law (over 70 years) and the focus of the new regulations, there remains a dearth of knowledge and an abundance of misconceptions. The result is that a number of exchanges are not structured properly or are not utilized where they could be. The 1031 Exchange is a unique and intricate tax technique in which qualified intermediaries are a natural resource. They can provide the essential expertise that ensures that this wealth accumulation strategy is performed properly and often.

1031s Are Not Just for Limiting Taxes—There Are Other Benefits

The one thing that 1031 Exchanges are designed to accomplish is avoiding taxes.

But budding real estate pros can turn to 1031 Exchanges to carry out a variety of business strategies. A retail owner, for example, might use a 1031 Exchange to trade an old mall for a newer, trendier shopping center. In a more complex deal, an Exchange can be part of an exit strategy for a partnership.

In a 1031 Exchange, owners defer the capital gains tax they typically would pay in a property sale. For instance, a new real estate pro that purchases a building for $2 million and then sells it for $5 million will defer paying taxes on the $3 million gain.

Section 1031 Exchanges do wonders for the economy. They spur development, generate jobs, create wealth, and allow people to increase their net worth. They do not, in and of themselves, deprive the government of tax revenue.

While policymakers and tax experts wrestle with reforming the tax code to make it fairer and simpler, section 1031 stands as an example of a tax policy that really works.

It permits those newly minted real estate pros, even those with only modest amounts of capital, to transform themselves into financially successful and secure people, with positive ripple effects throughout the economy.

Karl R. Foust, a business development consultant with qualified intermediary Bayview Financial Exchange Services of Miami, Florida, offers three examples of different kinds of 1031 transactions.

Each of the scenarios can have dozens of variations and in each scenario, the focus is to reinvest with the developer, but, as Foust points out, they do not necessarily have to.

Scenario 1: Assignment of contract for a gain.

Exchanger has contracted and deposited $100,000 with developer for Condo A toward a purchase price of $500,000. Exchanger wishes to purchase a different unit(s) with developer and the developer had a new buyer for Condo A. New purchase price of Condo A is $700,000. Exchanger assigns contract to new buyer, who must pay $300,000 toward the purchase up front ($100,000 original deposit plus $200,000 gain). At that time exchanger opens 1031 Exchange, deposits the $300,000 (less fees to broker and developer) with QI Bayview 1031. At this point the developer still has $100,000 on deposit, but the closing price on Condo A has changed from $500,000 to $700,000. Exchanger then has 45 days to choose where to invest the $300,000. If exchanger chooses to invest in new condo contract(s) with original developer, as a motivating factor developer may apply the fee toward this deposit. Exchanger may, however, choose to pay the fee and invest elsewhere.

Assuming that the replacement unit(s) is comparable to the original, exchanger will exit one condo contract and end up with two (or three), still with the original deposit of $100,000.

Scenario 2:
Developer resells the property and gain is taken at move-in.

Developer approaches existing clients with the proposal to invest in other condo units. Developer grants an option contract on new unit(s). Developer then markets original unit for sale at the new price. When sale is consummated (property is ready for move-in), the gain and original deposit go into a 1031 Exchange with Bayview 1031, and then the original client (exchanger) reinvests all the proceeds into the new contracts (exercises the options). Fee structure will need to be worked out between the original buyer and the developer.

In both of these cases, a fee contract will need to be worked out up front for bringing this concept to fruition. A flat fee or a percentage would certainly be in order. Bayview should not be a part of that since the qualified intermediary must remain independent. The qualified intermediary only effects the transaction.

Scenario 3: Exchanger holds contract until closing, then assigns to actual buyer during simultaneous close.

The investor has entered into a preconstruction contract with a developer. At least one year has passed. Exchanger desires to take the gain on the contract and buy something different or contract for another preconstruction property(s). Broker or developer brings new buyer who replaces deposit. When the unit is ready for closing (move-in), the deposit, which was replaced, must be transferred back via builder or closing agent and into QI. At closing, contract is transferred to new buyer before title passes. Simultaneously, the actual buyer purchases at the price plus the markup.

Recently a ruling emerged from a case involving the IRS permitting the taxpayer to exchange contracts to purchase (preconstruction) or an option for real property and/or vice versa.

At least one financial exchange service announced that it would perform the exchange as long as a client had already sought an opinion from his or her tax adviser. The ruling from the IRS decreed that when anyone does an exchange, the IRS might question it and get a ruling: one district might rule one way; another district, another way.

Exchange services executives expressed confidence that real estate is a bundle of rights: when someone has a contract to purchase real estate, it may take that person three years to close on real estate; but the client had purchased the contract three years earlier and so the contract can increase in value.

The same principle applied to real estate. The IRS determined (in Revenue Ruling 84-121 [1984-2 C.B. 168, 1984-33 I.R.B. 4]) that an option was indeed a bundle of rights and, therefore, could be used to do an exchange for property that already existed. Along with the *Starker* case, this ruling prompted the viewpoint that a bundle of rights under an existing contract on a piece of property that is not completed can be exchanged for a piece of property that already has been completed. ("Completed" means developed, constructed, or finished.) These rulings make it easier for qualified intermediaries to take the position that "contract for contract" is a valid like-kind exchange.

The client could probably sell the contract for $1 million during the three years and take the profit. The key IRS change is that before this time, a contract to purchase did not represent real estate because the client didn't own it; the client had to close the contract before doing a 1031—the client had to actually own the real estate itself. The ruling states that a contract equates with ownership. Now all a client has to do, which one could not do before this ruling, is to do a 1031 when selling a contract. The client can take the proceeds and reinvest in a like-kind exchange. In real estate everything is considered like kind. The client does not have to hold the contract until he or she closes on the contract; the client can do a 1031 earlier, which means that he or she can increase the assets early.

The new IRS ruling opens up a large market for real estate investors.

CHAPTER 13

1031 Exchanges and the Importance of Deadlines

There are a few IRS guidelines you must follow to take part in a legal tax-free exchange.

All 1031 Exchanges revolve around two absolute deadlines. The first is the 45-day rule. Within 45 days of closing on the relinquished property, a 1031 trader must file a list of possible replacement properties with a qualified intermediary—a firm certified to act as the closing agent for 1031 Exchanges.

Most who fail to qualify run afoul of the 45-day rule. The exchanger has 45 days after the close of escrow to disclose up to three prospective replacement properties and has up to 180 days to close escrow on a replacement property (after you notify the QI that you have identified the property).

If you are doing this in the middle of filing a tax return, you can get an extension on the tax return, otherwise you will lose the advantage of the tax gain.

Also, a "qualified intermediary" must handle the exchange transaction. Per IRS code, a qualified intermediary can be anyone with the exception of the exchanger's attorney, banker, certified public accountant, employee, or family member. Miss either deadline, the one of 45 days or the one of 180 days, and the IRS will send a capital gains tax bill.

In light of the deadlines and other issues that can complicate 1031 Exchanges, a cottage industry of 1031 Exchange advisors has emerged over the years. These advisors include qualified intermediaries, who provide technical advice and closing services. Numerous real estate brokers and net-leasing firms help exchangers locate replacement properties, and accountants and attorneys provide specialized tax advice related to 1031 transactions.

The larger and more complex the 1031 transaction, the more important comprehensive expertise becomes. One 1031 Exchange adviser even suggested that negotiating a 1031 Exchange can cause brain damage, because one can never be sure any particular deal will close. He was joking about the brain damage—but not about the uncertainty of completing a deal.

Sometimes, a seller tries to use the 180-day deadline as leverage to raise the price of the property. For that reason, it is unwise to be in a situation where you have to close on a particular property to protect your tax position.

1031s and Partnerships

The 1031 Exchange strategy gets more complicated when business strategies involve partnerships. You cannot exchange partnership interests in the 1031 market. But the partnership itself can make an exchange.

If a two-person partnership owned a single property worth $10 million, the partnership could enter the exchange market and trade it for two properties worth $10 million.

Those properties could match the partners' interests and allow for a convenient dissolution of the partnership in the future. This is a partnership exit strategy called "swap and drop."

In a 1031 Exchange, real estate owners can defer the tax on the disposition of an appreciated property by acquiring a like-kind replacement property for investment or business use.

In these exchanges, business or investment property is disposed of through a qualified intermediary, and the proceeds are used to purchase a replacement property of like kind.

This results in a deferral of all or most of the gain that otherwise would be subject to income tax on the disposed property. The replacement property has a carryover tax basis that is generally the value of the replacement property less the gain deferred in the exchange.

As the Internal Revenue Code's Section 1031 becomes more widely known across the country, many early-stage real estate pros are discovering its advantages.

Yet some investors incorrectly believe that a section 1031 tax-deferred exchange is a tax avoidance device for large corporations. This lack of understanding has the effect of undermining one of the tax code's most effective components.

In a 1031 Exchange, real property must be replaced with like-kind property in order to defer the gain. Properties are of like kind if they are of the same nature or character, even if they differ in grade or quality. Personal properties of a like class are like-kind properties.

Like-kind property exchanges are more and more popular. Falling under section 1031 of the tax code, like-kind property exchanges offer business owners or investors a way to trade their property for something of similar value without reporting a profit and, thereby, defer paying taxes on the gain.

It could be a chicken farm or a piece of rental property that is the focus of the 1031 Exchange. With intangible property, it might be a company vehicle or a piece of machinery, though these can present a serious problem for business owners because the depreciation on equipment is much faster than on real estate. One might be able to write off the entire value of a computer system in two years, so even if you sell it for less than you paid for it, it would still appear as a gain on your taxes.

Federal law determines the definition of real and personal property for tax depreciation purposes.

Federal law tends to classify fixtures in a building as real property. Therefore, property such as wall coverings, carpeting, special-purpose wiring, or other installations affixed to the building can be considered real property under state law and like kind for section 1031 purposes, but personal property in cost segregation studies.

Thus, investors can benefit from both the gain deferral under section 1031 for real estate exchanges and the enhanced cost recovery deductions of a cost segregation study.

It was the *Starker* decision that made life easier for the new real estate pro. Now when you sell a piece of property, the money doesn't go to you, it goes to a middleman, the qualified intermediary.

For real estate investors, the 1991 codifications created a brand new market that, fortunately for everyone, allowed this new class of real estate entrepreneurs to emerge. Many entrepreneurs have taken modest investments and made themselves multimillionaires.

One such example that we came across involved a 1031 Exchange. In the 1970s, Mr. Smith bought a vacant lot in the Far West listed at $3,000. He put down $300 and the seller agreed to finance the $2,700 balance. The next year, he took the same trip, visited his lot, and found the neighboring one for sale by the same seller and at the same price and terms.

So he bought the second lot, too.

About 10 years later he was offered $30,000 each for his Far

West lots, which would give him $60,000 to invest in other real estate. That, however, would make him liable for approximately $15,000 in capital gains taxes if he sold the lots outright.

Upon a financial adviser's instructions, Mr. Smith decided to conduct a 1031 tax-deferred Exchange. His realtor found two duplexes at $30,000 each. The person who wanted his Far West lots purchased the two duplexes and then exchanged them for his two lots, thereby completing a 1031 Exchange. Mr. Smith later refinanced his duplexes for $42,000. With the $40,000 cash left after closing costs, he purchased a $225,000 warehouse.

In 1989, he refinanced the warehouse, by then worth $450,000, to get $115,000 in cash for the down payment on a $350,000 single-family residence. In 1999, he exchanged the warehouse for a small office building in Hawaii, once again deferring all taxes on his gains. And in 2000, Mr. Smith sold his home for $875,000.

He applied Internal Revenue Code Section 121, which allows a $500,000-per-couple exemption. Hence, his taxes on the residential sale were a mere $3,750.

The man still owns the two duplexes, now valued at $100,000 each. His net worth is close to $2.9 million. If both he and his wife were to die today, their estates would owe no estate taxes. All of this began with a pair of $3,000 lots, each purchased for only $300 down.

The objective of the 1031 is this: the investor can use it to accumulate wealth by deferring the taxes and by using 100 cents on a dollar. This is in contrast to paying capital gains tax or ordinary income taxes. Five years ago 1031 Exchanges were used only for investment property and for property held in trade or business.

There is another advantage to a 1031 Exchange: You are getting an interest-free loan from the IRS. When you paid taxes the money went to the government. When you do a 1031 you can use money in your new property.

Five years ago you might've bought an investment property for $250,000. Today you can sell it at $1.5 million. If you had to pay the tax on capital gains, which has been as high as 25% but is 15% today, you would've owed $187,500 to the government.

At 25% down—that is $187,500 times 4—you have almost $750,000 worth of buying power. If you took the money you saved and bought a house, putting down 25% (and most only require between 5% and 10% down), you could purchase $750,000 of property with the money you save by not paying the IRS.

There is, of course, a downside to using the 1031 Exchange: ultimately, you have to pay the deferred tax sometime in the future.

If you continue to defer for the next 30 years and you happen to die, the law says that you have $1.5 million of exemptions in taxes if you are single and $3 million if you're married. That is, if you have accumulated $3.5 million in deferred capital gains and you owe the government $3 million, your estate gets the exemption. Your heirs owe only $500,000 out of the $3.5 million in tax bill.

And your heirs inherit the property that you own now at this stepped-up value. Once the heirs own the property and want to sell the property, they can continue the 1031 process.

The capital gains tax is at 15%. When it was at 25% it was much more advantageous to do a 1031 Exchange.

If you're in a state with state taxes like New York, you cannot defer the state taxes under a 1031 Exchange and you also have what's called a "depreciation recapture tax." This means that if you depreciated a building over ten years and haven't completed the depreciation at the time of the sale, you have to pay a depreciation recapture tax at 25%.

Other reasons to do 1031s: You may own a piece of raw acreage, on which you are not getting any depreciation at all. But you can exchange that raw acreage for an apartment building and now get the tax write-offs.

Find Good Help

1031 Exchanges are still an unknown strategy in many parts of the country and the word "exchange" gives the false impression of inflexible barter and other false negative connotations. As with all marketing ventures and new service offerings, be sure you are in compliance with the rules of professional conduct and ethics of your State Board of Accountancy.

There is a downside to relying upon 1031 Exchanges. You never know what the future will bring. The government might decide one day that it needs the money it is losing from these Exchanges. The government could get rid of the 1031 Exchange code and require a capital gains tax bill on each of these transactions.

Let's face it. There is a large loss in tax revenue in this program that benefits the very few—usually the wealthier segments of society. If the national debt moves ahead toward record highs, the government may come under increasing pressure to find additional financing.

No less a figure than the former Federal Reserve Board Chairman Alan Greenspan has weighed in by saying that, "reducing the federal debt to the public at this stage is unquestionably the most important thing that I believe we can do if meeting the future needs of the economy is the standard."

We here in Florida are very lucky. We don't have a state income tax per se. There are many states that have a state income tax along with federal taxes. And in addition if you had a piece of property that you had taken depreciation on, you would have to pay another tax, the depreciation recapture.

STRATEGY #26:
BE AN INVESTOR, NOT A DEALER.

How often can you do a 1031 Exchange? Is there any IRS stipulation limiting them?

The answer: You can do it over and over and over again.

But the IRS wants to see that you are an investor, not a "dealer." It doesn't want to see you buying a piece of property today and one month later selling it. It considers that dealing, not investing.

If you've done three or four 1031 Exchanges in a year, you're questionable to the IRS. If you've done one or two, you may be questionable but you are not as questionable as someone who's done three or four.

Here's a case where the IRS challenged one man's categorizing the sale as a 1031 Exchange. Mr. Jones bought a $1 million plot on the Pacific Ocean. He had plans to build a 7,500-square-foot house on it and rent it out for $25,000 a month. (This was a number of years ago.) He had his plans, his permits. On day one he started building. Three months later someone came along and bought this partially developed property for over $2 million, giving him a $1 million profit.

Now if you're an investor one goal is to make money. Mr. Jones contended that it was not his intent to sell this property right away—he hadn't put up a for sale sign, or advertised—but the buyer came out of the blue. Mr. Jones won his case.

You might convince the IRS that its challenge is wrong on other grounds as well—one of them is "changed circumstance."

You could buy an office building and it remains empty. No matter what you have tried to do you have not been successful in getting tenants into the building. You'd be a stupid investor to keep building for a long time if you can't get tenants. So changed circumstances would be another valid reason to sell within a short period of time.

STRATEGY #27:
USE THESE STRATEGIES ON MULTIPLE PROPERTIES.

Can you do multiple properties or does it have to be one property for that $1 million?

Answer: You can buy as many properties as you want.

You may have heard about the three-property rule, which means you're limited to purchasing three properties. That's not true. The three-property rule says you can identify any three that you want at any value.

Then there is the 200% rule. It says you can identify as many properties as you want, but altogether their value can't equal more than 200% of what you just sold. So if you sold for $1 million and you identified seven properties, all seven together couldn't equal more than $2 million.

Then there's the 95% rule, which I've never seen used in real estate. It says you can identify as many properties as you want, we don't care what the value is, but you must purchase 95% of the value of what you identified. That's very hard to do in a real estate transaction.

More and more people are getting involved in 1031 Exchanges. We've come across many accountants and attorneys who are not very knowledgeable about how to do a 1031 Exchange, so make sure the people you hire are knowledgeable.

CHAPTER 14

Save Taxes and Improve Cash Flow: Do a Cost Segregation Study

STRATEGY #28:
TO SHELTER LARGE AMOUNTS OF MONEY FROM TAX
LIABILITY, ENGAGE IN A COST SEGREGATION STUDY.

Tax-deferral strategies are a great way to minimize taxes, and cost segregation and section 1031 Exchanges are two of the most valuable tax-deferral strategies available to commercial real estate owners today. We've dealt with 1031 Exchange programs in the previous two chapters. Now we turn to cost segregation analysis.

New investors are improving cash flow and finding immediate tax savings from their business properties by utilizing this specialized depreciation program called cost segregation. It's a program we are increasingly advising new real estate pros to employ.

A cost segregation study (CSS) is the process of reviewing the costs a taxpayer incurs to acquire, construct, or improve real estate. It identifies the specific types of assets being placed in service and often leads to a cost allocation that assigns part of the cost to personal property.

In a section 1031 Exchange, real property must be replaced with real property in order to defer the gain. In general, state law determines the definition of real property under section 1031. In contrast, the definition of real and personal property for tax depreciation purposes is determined under federal law. State law tends to classify fixtures in a building as real property. Therefore, property such as wall coverings, carpeting, special-purpose wiring, or other installations affixed to the building can be considered real property under state law and like kind for section 1031 purposes, but personal property in cost segregation studies. Thus, real estate owners can benefit from both the gain deferral under section 1031 for real estate exchanges and the enhanced cost recovery deductions of the cost segregation study.

Cost segregation brings a great IRS-recognized tax savings strategy to commercial property owners interested in retaining cash.

When investing in real estate, many people lose sight of the fact that a property has numerous components, making it one of the most unique investment vehicles available.

With cost segregation you depreciate more of the property over a shorter period of time. With a cost segregation study, you depreciate more of this property over a shorter period of time.

Cost segregation can be complex because the tax laws provide many different asset lives and categories that may be applicable to a building project.

Normally, when you build a building the general contractor provides you with a monthly draw request. In this draw request the contractor combines different construction costs into single line item categories (i.e., concrete, plumbing, electrical, etc.). These categories have numerous components. For example, the electrical contract might have light fixtures, panel boards, conduit and wiring, etc., buried within the single line item. Once the building is completed, you give your project-related construction costs to your accountant to prepare your depreciation schedules and tax returns.

Since the contractor didn't break out the different components of the building, the accountant is hard pressed to identify the different components of the building. Therefore, the accountant usually places the entire project-related construction costs into a long tax life, typically 39 years (nonresidential real property).

Construction-related soft costs historically have been lumped together as part of real property. However, with cost segregation, these soft costs can be allocated to various components of the property, many of which have shorter depreciable lives than the real property component. The result is a faster write-off of costs previously included as real property.

Cost segregation has been around since the 1960s in one form or another. It has been called component depreciation, an investment tax credit, and various other names. The primary goal of cost segregation is to identify building components that can be reclassified from real property to personal property. This goal results in a substantially shorter depreciable tax life and accelerated depreciation methods.

Cost segregation is a strategic tax savings tool that permits companies and individuals to increase their cash flow by accelerating depreciation expense (i.e., 5- and 7-year personal property and 15-year land improvements/real property). Ordinarily, the cost of real or section 1250 property is recovered over lengthy periods (27.5 and 39 years for residential and nonresidential property, respectively), using the straight-line method of depreciation. Personal, or section 1245 property is recovered over considerably shorter periods (5, 7, or 15 years), and employs accelerated ("front-end loaded") methods of depreciation, such as 200% or 150% declining balance.

The problem arises when you're doing a straight-line depreciation on a commercial property or an investment property other than residential—residential is 27.5 years, commercial property is 39 years. So when you buy a commercial property and you depreciate that over 39 years you are depreciating that over a long period of time. So you're losing the value of that depreciation because you can't use it unless you own the property for 39 years; then you would get the full value of that depreciation

Cost segregation and 1031 Exchanges are not mutually exclusive. It is possible to use both in the same transaction. A 1031 Exchange is used as the result of a sale of a property. Cost segregation is used upon the purchase of a property.

Sheltering Income

Cost segregation studies can be performed on purchased or newly constructed buildings. Studies can be performed for buildings placed in service as far back as 1987, even if the year is "closed" for tax purposes. Recently issued IRS revenue procedures permit taxpayers who have claimed less than the allowable depreciation to claim the omitted amount over a four-year period. In addition, the segregated components continue to be depreciated over shorter lives from then on.

Real estate owners and investors can use cost segregation studies to accelerate overall property depreciation, which can produce a current income tax benefit. This tax benefit applies to commercial, industrial, multifamily, and special-purpose real estate. Typically, the more specialized and costly the property, the greater the tax benefits. Often, these benefits are neither captured nor maximized by many real estate owners, because they neglect to have a cost segregation study done on their property.

A cost-segregation study is an asset-reclassification strategy that accelerates tax depreciation deductions. Simply put, certain real estate is reclassified from long-lived real property to shorter-lived personal property for depreciation purposes. Depreciation deductions for the personal property then can be greatly accelerated, producing greater present-value tax savings.

An analysis of costs can be conducted from either detailed construction records, when such records are available, or by using qualified appraisers, architects, or engineers to perform the allocation analysis. In both instances, a tax expert also is needed to identify the types of property that can qualify as short-lived assets and can be segregated from long-lived assets.

Under prior law taxpayers would separate a building's parts into its various components—doors, walls, and floors. Once these components were isolated, taxpayers would depreciate them using a short cost-recovery period. CPAs referred to this practice as component depreciation. The introduction of the accelerated cost recovery system (ACRS) and the modified accelerated cost recovery system (MACRS) eliminated the use of component depreciation, but not the use of cost segregation.

The legislation and procedures used in engineering-based cost segregation studies have been around since the enactment of the Investment Tax Credit (ITC) in 1962. It had been possible prior to 1986 to front-load the depreciation on an apartment complex to get 200% of the losses of the depreciation in one year; this made real estate a tax shelter.

With the repeal of the ITC and the enactment of the rules limiting passive losses in 1986, most companies assumed that engineering-based cost segregation provided no further benefit under the new tax law. However, in a 1997 tax court case involving Hospital Corporation of America, the taxpayer successfully defended the application of engineering-based costs.

The IRS now has acquiesced to the viability of engineering-based cost segregation as a legitimate method to differentiate real and personal property under current tax law.

In it the Tax Court permitted HCA to use cost segregation with respect to a multitude of improvements.

Critical to the Tax Court's analysis was that in formulating accelerated depreciation methods Congress intended to distinguish between components that constitute IRC section 1250 class property (real property) and property items that constitute section 1245 class property (tangible personal property).

This distinction opened the doors to cost segregation.

Armed with this victory, taxpayers have increasingly begun to use cost segregation to their advantage. The IRS reluctantly agreed that cost segregation does not constitute component depreciation. Moreover, cost segregation recently was featured in temporary regulations issued by the Treasury Department.

In a chief counsel advisory (CCA), however, the IRS warned taxpayers that an "accurate cost segregation study may not be based on noncontemporaneous records, reconstructed data or taxpayers' estimates or assumptions that have no supporting records."

STRATEGY #29:
TO DEFER THE MAXIMUM AMOUNT OF INCOME TAX, COMBINE COST SEGREGATION ANALYSIS WITH A 1031 EXCHANGE.

Combining cost segregation and 1031 Exchanges allows newly minted real estate pros to defer the maximum amount of income taxes. Using cost segregation on replacement property acquired in 1031 Exchanges, budding real estate pros can reclassify real property as personal property in order to obtain faster depreciation write-offs. This is a particularly good option if the owner is exchanging up in value.

However, in certain situations cost segregation may give rise to depreciation recapture as ordinary income in otherwise nontaxable exchanges, and considering that most accountants have no idea what cost segregation analysis is, you must be very careful whom you hire to represent you.

Depreciating Items in the Property

If you own five condominiums, you can lump them together and actually do cost segregation.

Cost segregation enables you to offset passive income with passive losses. So if you have a property you've owned for some time and its generating income but you no longer have a depreciable base, you can now buy another property. You can use a cost segregation study to increase the losses on the new property to offset the taxable income on the older property.

People say real estate is still one of the best legal tax shelters once you understand the methodology in how to improve and increase that depreciation. Now you can do this with new or existing property. Cost segregation applies to new construction purchases, leasehold improvements, exhausted property, 1031s, and inherited property.

If a budding real estate pro acquired a commercial property or improved a commercial property since 1987, and he or she has a cost basis of at least $500,000 and plans to own the property for at least three years, he/she can benefit from additional depreciation deductions using cost segregation.

One of the big advantages is this: assume you own multiple condo units. You can depreciate—you can kind of lump them together—and componentize those particular units. Component depreciation allows taxpayers to depreciate structural components separately—based on the useful life of the component.

The component that you plan to use has to be a property attached to the building, not something that you could remove that easily.

The IRS has come out with some rulings supporting cost segregation analysis.

One example: In a typical medical facility using the 200% declining-balance method, with a 6% discount rate, the distinction means a present-value difference in the value of deductions of nearly 47% of original cost.

In other words, under former tax credit rules regarding the definition of section 38 property, certain costs, which have been classified as real property, and are subject to 39 years depreciable life, should be classified as personal property subject to 5, 7, or 15 years depreciable life.

That means you can reclassify the roof, the windows, the studs, the sheet rock, the floors, the paint that has a useful life (but it doesn't last 39 years), the parking lot, and much more. When you start to itemize all these items—and there could be thousands of them—you now change the life factor of these particular components.

As a result, you now shift that depreciation from the 39 years—you bring it forward. You wind up with a higher loss factor in the early years. What does that mean for you?

If you have income from other properties or if you are considered a real estate professional for IRS purposes, and you have income from other sources, you can take the losses from a real estate transaction and offset them against that other gain or ordinary income.

If you have money earning from something else, and you wish to be classified as a real estate professional, you must have worked 750 hours a year in real estate.

Each item of property is assigned one of the following classes:

- 3-year property
- 5-year property (asset class 57.0)
- 7-year property
- 14-year land improvement
- 20-year property

- 27.5-year residential real property
- 31.5/39-year nonresidential real property

One can use the figure $10 million. The number is irrelevant; it's the concept that matters. This is the depreciable cost basis for your property minus the land.

The current cost of property is $10 million. The percentage of property assigned to a shorter depreciable life is zero.

As a result of the cost segregation study, the depreciation in the first year is $400,000. So 40% of the value of the building is going to be recharactierized and changes the depreciable base. You'll change $4 million to a ten-year basis.

The initial depreciation using 39 years on the $10 million was $256,000. The new estimated depreciation is $706,000. So there is a net difference of $450,000. This gives an estimated cash tax savings of $180,000.

You've done nothing different. All you did was analyze it better.

If you sell the property you can do a 1031 Exchange and then once you die, you eliminate the taxes. When you die that depreciable base goes back up to the new value at the time of your demise. So in other words, you eliminate it. If you depreciated this over a five- or ten-year period, and you then die, the property, if valued at $20 million, starts off a new tax basis for your heirs.

What can your heirs do at that point? They can do it all over again.

Use Cost Segregation to Exchange Up

Cost segregation studies are most useful when the taxpayer is exchanging up in value significantly, or exchanging from nondepreciable property, such as land, to depreciable property.

For example, installed carpet purchased with a facility is considered personal property for depreciation purposes and recovered in a five- or seven-year period using the 200% declining balance method of depreciation. If this is not done, the carpet would be included in the value of the real property and its cost would be capitalized and recovered on a straight-line basis over 39 years.

Land improvements, however, remain section 1250 property (real property). Section 1245 property (personal property) has significant depreciation recapture rules in a section 1031 Exchange; generally the replacement property must contain the same value of section 1245 property as the relinquished property, or the taxpayer will recapture the difference (up to the realized amount) at ordinary income tax rates.

As an example, Joan, the owner of a manufacturing facility, had a cost segregation study performed in 2000 that reclassified $1 million of real property as section 1245 property. In 2004, after realizing the benefits from $430,000 of depreciation deductions, Joan exchanged the facility for an office building of equal value and equity.

Since the section 1245 property in the relinquished property still is valued at $1 million, Joan typically would pay no tax on the exchange.

However, the office building has only $700,000 of section 1245 property; the remaining $300,000 of value is section 1250 property. Therefore, Joan will recapture and pay ordinary income tax on $300,000 of the prior depreciation deductions due to the difference between the $1 million of section 1245 property in the relinquished property and the $700,000 of section 1245 property in the replacement property.

Despite the potential of future taxes in a section 1031 Exchange, cost segregation still can be justified due to the increase in present value of the accelerated depreciation deductions. Based on the fundamental principle of the time value of money, a dollar saved today through reduced taxes always is worth more than a dollar in later years. Furthermore, Joan could have exchanged into other real property with similar amounts of personal section 1245 property and avoided the recapture tax altogether.

Engineering-based cost segregation studies take assets that have been classified as real property for federal income tax purposes and, using engineering-based analysis techniques, reclassify the property that should have been classified as personal property into the shorter, appropriate class lives. The engineering-based cost segregation study provides tax preparers with the information and supporting documentation needed to depreciate assets over the appropriate, shorter tax lives.

Real property recovery periods range from 27.5 to 39 years and employ the straight-line method of depreciation. Personal property can be depreciated in as few as five years and employ a 200% or 150% declining balance method of depreciation. The result is an increase in current year depreciation expense due to a significantly shorter depreciable tax life and a front-end-loaded method of calculating the depreciation expense. The resulting increase in depreciation expense typically yields a significant decrease in income tax liability.

A good cost segregation firm brings engineering, accounting, and tax expertise together in a unique marriage to ensure maximum benefit for the property owner. This expertise also ensures that the engineering study will be delivered in an understandable, supportable, and technically sound format.

In Chapter 4 of the IRS Cost Segregation Audit Techniques Guide, the first element of a "quality cost segregation study" is "preparation by an individual with expertise and experience."

The Audit Techniques Guide goes on to say: "Preparation of cost segregation studies requires knowledge of both the construction process and the tax law involving property classifications for depreciation purposes. In general, a study by a construction engineer is more reliable than one conducted by someone with no engineering or construction background. Experience in cost estimating and allocation, as well as knowledge of the applicable law, are other important criteria."

A Unique Marriage

Cost segregation methods employed nationally vary greatly in their detail and scope. Cost segregation professionals need to spend several hours, even days in some cases, at the site verifying the accuracy of blueprints and specifications or taking necessary measurements to calculate an asset's costs and segregate them. Selecting a firm that uses qualified professionals with years of significant, relevant experience can be an important differentiator in the quality of a cost segregation study.

In this example we see the tax benefits of cost segregation.

A company constructed an $11 million skilled nursing facility in 1988. During the first ten years of operation, depreciation expense was calculated as $3.3 million. As a result of a cost segregation study performed in 1998, the company was able to increase its depreciation expense by more than $1.6 million during the next four years. This increase produced discounted present-value tax savings and additional cash flow of more than $340,000 for the company.

In another example, another property acquired in 1987 cost less than $1 million. Additions worth more than $8 million were added from 1992 through 1997. As originally calculated, the depreciation expense from 1987 to 1998 was $3 million. In 1999, a cost segregation study identified items such as land improvements, kitchen and medical-related equipment, decorative millwork, wall coverings, telecommunications wiring, and emergency generators as personal property, resulting in an increase in depreciation expense of $1.3 million. This reclassification of property resulted in discounted present-value tax savings and additional cash flow of more than $280,000 to the facility's owner.

When Should You Begin a Cost Segregation Study?

The ideal time to begin a cost segregation study is when plans to construct, remodel, or expand an existing building, or to purchase a building, are first drafted. Ideally, the cost segregation study should be completed during the year the building is placed in service.

If you didn't complete a cost segregation study when the building was first placed in service a cost segregation study can still be performed. Recent IRS procedures make it easier for you to go backwards, allowing you to change your accounting method as far back as 1987 without filing an amended tax return. You can recapture all of the understated depreciation expense for any asset that has been improperly classified in previous years. Here's an example.

Let's say you placed an asset in service in 1990. The cost of the asset is $100,000, the tax life you gave this asset is 27.5 years—and the depreciation method was straight-line. The asset has been depreciating for ten years (approximately 32% depreciated). The remaining basis of this asset is $68,000. The correct life of this asset should have been five years.

The IRS states that if you have truly made a classification error, as in this case, you can make a correction to this asset without being penalized. Therefore, you can bring forward that understated depreciation expense ($68,000) in the year that you are requesting the change in accounting method. According to the IRS, the understated depreciation expense deduction must be prorated over a four-year period beginning with the year of change.

To determine whether you might qualify for this change in accounting method procedure, first look at your depreciation schedule. If you placed a building in service prior to 2000 and the entire project cost of the building (real property only) is sitting at a 27.5- or 39-year life, you may want to look at having a cost segregation study done.

What Does a Cost Segregation Study Entail?

A cost segregation study is a comprehensive analysis of the total cost or value of building and site improvements. Cost segregation studies typically do not include analyzing the value of land, furniture, fixtures, and equipment. These studies apportion the value or cost of all specific components of the building and site improvements to certain specific federal tax depreciable-life categories.

To optimize the reclassification from longer lives to shorter lives, a detailed analysis of the property is required. Qualified engineers and appraisers typically perform these analyses. An understanding of specific tax guidelines and regulations, tax court cases, revenue rulings, and current legislation is required to conduct such studies. Cost segregation studies should be utilized for any taxpayer who constructs a building, acquires a property, expands an existing facility, or changes the tax basis of real property.

In addition, cost segregation studies can be conducted on properties constructed or acquired in the past, even if no cost segregation study was performed at the time the property was placed in service.

Generally, cost segregation methodology requires establishing a complete and thorough understanding of the total cost or value of the real estate asset in order to determine the total depreciable tax basis.

In new construction, further details of construction cost information, both direct and indirect, are typically utilized for the building. "Direct costs" are costs for labor and materials necessary to construct the asset. "Indirect costs" are items that are required for the project, but not directly associated with specific labor and materials. Some examples of indirect costs include architectural and engineering design fees, contractor overhead and profit, permit fees, and construction interest. These indirect costs are allocated to direct costs on a pro rata basis.

Next, the cost segregation analyst inspects the property to gain a full comprehension of the function, nature, and operation of the various building components. The analyst must also confirm the accuracy of the construction or property documents. This is critical in determining the specific property classifications that are associated with depreciable federal tax lives. It establishes appropriate property units by asset function.

The central and most significant step in the cost segregation study is the specific identification and quantification of the asset components that qualify for 5-, 7-, or 15-year depreciable tax lives. Often, for newly built property, detailed construction cost information can provide a breakdown of the various costs.

A cost segregation study analyzes and supplements the cost information with "quantity take-off estimates" that serve to reclassify even more property into a shorter tax life. Quantity take-off estimating must follow generally accepted engineering and cost estimating procedures. These procedures include the estimation of material and labor quantities and the determination of cost estimates from recognized construction estimating sources or other supportable sources.

The last step in a cost segregation study is to document and report the findings. Generally, the identification and quantification process is supported with documentation and calculations. These are typically referenced by use of an automated, computer-based cost segregation report. This report provides a description of the property, the steps taken to determine the quantification and property life determination, and the supporting detail.

The analysis procedures require that a consistent, logical, and supportable report be produced. There are a number of other supporting and related calculations that are also part of the process. A well-conducted study always includes a detailed, referenced, work paper file, which supports the final conclusions of the study, and also provides an audit trail. When similar property portfolios exist, a sampling methodology may be applied to support the analysis.

As part of MACRS, nonresidential real properties are depreciated over 39 years via straight-line depreciation. Some assets, which are often classified as real property, however, may be depreciated over five or seven years, if they are nonstructural components.

These assets are defined under section 1245(a)(3) of the Internal Revenue Code as "Personal Property." Yet, there is no specific definition of "personal property." Treas. Reg. [sections] 1.48-1(c) defines the term "tangible personal property" as "any tangible property except land and improvements thereto, such as buildings and other inherently permanent structures, including items which are structural components of such buildings or structures." Several factors were determined in *Whiteco Industries, Inc. v. Commissioner,* 65 T.C. 664 (1975), to constitute whether property is inherently permanent. These factors include:

• Movability of the property
• Permanency of design or construction
• Expected length of affixation
• Significance of removal
• Extent of damage if removed
• Manner of affixation
• Reusability of the property

When section 1250 property is reallocated to section 1245, the differences can be great. It takes a unique combination of engineering and tax expertise to properly analyze, as we've noted earlier, construction information, compute industry-standard estimates, and identify and segregate the subcomponent costs needed for cost segregation, however. CPAs without that expertise might consider hiring a consultant.

Tax advisers should alert taxpayers to the possibility of future depreciation recapture so they can anticipate paying some tax in the later exchange or making sure that the replacement property has sufficient amounts of section 1245 property to avoid recapture.

There also are recapture rules for section 1250 property in an exchange, but they are less onerous. Only the excess depreciation over straight-line depreciation (the additional depreciation) is subject to recapture. Land improvements such as sidewalks, fences, and landscaping are depreciated on an accelerated basis and can give rise to additional depreciation or recapture if the taxpayer does not acquire replacement property with an amount of section 1250 property equal to the additional depreciation.

For example, if you have $20,000 of additional depreciation from relinquished property disposition, you need to acquire only $20,000 of section 1250 property, including the building, to avoid recapture. Section 1250 recapture would be a problem, however, if you had additional depreciation and exchanges into raw land.

When combining tax-deferred exchanges under section 1031 and cost segregation, tax professionals must understand both the significant upside and the potential issues that are involved. With proper planning, using the two methods can provide a tremendous opportunity for taxpayers to defer income taxes into future periods and maximize cash flow in the current one through accelerated depreciation deductions.

PART VI

THE BUDDING REAL ESTATE PRO

CHAPTER 15

Personal Strategies for Real Estate Transactions

STRATEGY #30:
MAINTAIN FOCUS.

Many people who want to get into real estate have the desire, but they lack the follow-through to get the job done. They need focus.

The follow-through is all-important. Keep asking yourself: how am I going to get from one point to another? This is critical in the real estate business. Never lose focus.

What you need more than anything else in this business to succeed is commitment. That goes back to focus. If you have commitment you have focus, but you have to be prepared to make the commitment.

When people come to our seminars, and take an evening to listen to us and ask a question, that's a commitment. When people call us up on the phone and ask questions on our radio and television programs, that's a commitment. It means they are serious. They want to be successful; they want to learn something. They are prepared to make a commitment. They are on the right path to success.

STRATEGY #31:
AVOID BECOMING A JUMPER.

What, you ask, is a jumper?

It's someone who says: "I like this project. Let's go get this project." But then, all of a sudden, the person hears someone else say, "I just heard that this other project is coming out and they'll be offering this type of discount." He jumps into that project. And then, the person hears that someone else is offering another kind of project with unprecedented benefits. He jumps into this latter project. Before you know it we have a classic jumper.

The jumper goes from one project to another—where is his focus?

If you lose focus, if you become a jumper, you will lose in this game because you are going to come up against people like me, who have focus. I'll clean your clocks. That really is the secret—plain and simple.

If You Jump, You Lose

The card game poker is a game of focus. You think of where you want to go. You pay attention to what you're doing. Real estate is no different. They are both games. Real estate is also a game of focus. If you pay attention and put your mind to it, you will succeed.

Then there's knowledge. You've got to have knowledge—which is acquired through various means. One way is by networking. Another is by reading books or listening to tapes. A third is by attending seminars. But a fourth, and key way, is through experience.

Experience provides the best knowledge in the world. Listen to what people say. Surround yourself with professionals. If the people surrounding you know more than you, you acquire the knowledge faster.

STRATEGY #32:
SURROUND YOURSELF WITH PEOPLE WHO ARE SMARTER THAN YOU ARE.

One of the best secrets I've learned from being in this business for 35 years is this: I've always surrounded myself with people smarter than I am. All of my associates in the mortgage and real estate business are experienced real estate people, whether accountants, lawyers, or other kinds of professionals. Whenever they open their mouths, I listen.

STRATEGY #33:
DON'T BE CHEAP.

You cannot succeed in this business if you are cheap—plain and simple. I'm not saying you have to be irresponsible but when you go to hire a lawyer, when you walk into the law firm, if the first thing you ask a lawyer is how much do you charge, if the lawyer has any brains she'll throw you out of her office.

Because she will say to herself: "I need you like I need a hole in the head. All you are going to do, every time we need to do something, is to ask how much is this going to cost." So, spending to get what you need is not being irresponsible. It's a case of finding the professional that knows the business and paying whatever you must.

If you follow this advice, you will be a winner. You will get your money back a hundredfold. It's the person who's always looking for the angle, the cheap way out, who winds up with the lousy lawyers.

Believe me, I've come up against them. Whenever we're involved in litigation, we find out who are the lawyers on the other side, and I love the lawyers that people buy on the cheap. Put me against them—or put our lawyers against them—and we will win every time.

STRATEGY #34:
DON'T BE AFRAID OF LITIGATION.

If you're afraid of litigation, you better get out of the real estate business and find something else to do. There could be plenty of litigation that you have to endure. There could be plenty of litigation such as contract disputes, failure for sellers to provide adequate information, failure to implement what's promised in contracts.

Why invest in real estate? The answer, first and foremost, is for the preservation of capital. Does that mean you can't lose money? No, absolutely not. You can lose money in real estate just as easily as you can lose money by investing in any other investment vehicle.

The difference is that real estate is a more stable vehicle and the likelihood of losing all your money, or even some of your money, is a little more remote than if you're buying highly speculative stocks.

Real estate gives you numerous ways to protect the money that you have, as opposed to it just disappearing when the stock market suddenly drops 1,000 points—boom, it's gone.

Now, with real estate, I'm not saying the value of your assets can't go down but if it should happen, it won't be as fast and painful as with stocks that go sour. Because it takes a little time for real estate values to sink, investors can develop strategies to protect against getting too harmed.

One of the most important things about real estate is the opportunity it can give you to benefit from leverage. Those of you who are a bit cynical might say: Well, you're in the mortgage business, of course you're going to promote leverage. Okay, we confess that's true. But the fact is that you will make a higher return on your money utilizing the right kind of leveraged instrument than you will simply by using cash. I always tell people that if you have a lot of cash and you are going to take it to buy real estate, don't do it. Go buy a bond. Why knock yourself out? Why take any risk at all?

Cash Flow Is Crucial

In real estate, cash flow is crucial. What we're looking for in cash flow is a return on investment. If I have $1,000 and I get back $80 on that, my return on investment is 8%. That's very simple. With real estate, with the tax benefits associated with real estate, your return on investment and cash flow will increase, sometimes dramatically.

I love leverage. To me, leverage is what real estate is all about. If you understand leverage then you will understand how to make money in the real estate business. Unfortunately, most of the people in the real estate business are not savvy about leverage. In other words, they are not in the mortgage financing business. They have never been in that business.

What percentage of leverage is the best? It depends on the property, but typically you're looking at 80% loan-to-value ratio. Sometimes you can go higher. It all depends on what you do with the money. If you get a phone call from someone who tells you, "I can lend you 125% of the value of your house," then just hang up. Seriously, hang up. It's suicide.

If you needed 125% because your child needed an operation, that is a dire need. That is a desperate situation. Then I would say, "You've got to do what you've got to do."

But what you don't want to do is put yourself in a leveraged situation where you can't make a return on the money that you are borrowing. How do you achieve that return on investment? You take the money that you are borrowing from the real estate and invest it. What do we invest it in? More real estate is a pretty good idea. There are other choices—but whatever you do, don't buy depreciating assets.

For example, don't buy a car. You'd have to be nuts. Why would you leverage a house to buy a car? You get zero interest.

You want to learn how to use leverage. If you look at the purchase of property, the numbers are somewhat irrelevant. It's the philosophy and theory that is relevant. The numbers work kind of automatically. It almost doesn't matter what they are.

One of the things we do in our office is to make a great deal of effort and spend much time in educating our clients.

In talking about different kinds of mortgage programs, we talk about leveraging real estate: about how to use money. It's not just answering simple questions; you need to go into much more depth. If you look at the purchase of property, the numbers are somewhat irrelevant. It's the philosophy and theory that is relevant. The numbers work kind of automatically. It almost doesn't matter what the numbers are. Instead, look at what you can do using leverage and taking advantage of capital appreciation.

Use as an example a house that is purchased for $200,000 in an all-cash transaction. Let's say we buy the property with a 7% return and hold it for five years. On an annualized return, that would give us a compounded rate and return of $284,000. So your $200,000 investment at 7% return is worth $284,000. That's your return on investment—$84,000. In addition, if you were getting an 8% return on your money, that would be $16,000 a year. That represents about $80,000. Your total return of the $84,000 and the $80,000 is a total cash return of $164,000. What's your return on investment after five years? It's 82%.

An 82% return is a great investment. But, now one can use leverage.

Let's say you take a purchase price of $200,000 with a cash investment of 20% or $40,000. The loan amount is $160,000, which is 80% loan to value. The annualized return of 7% on

$200,000, the original purchase price, is $284,000. So the return on investment is $84,000 of appreciated value. In other words, $84,000 profit divided by the $40,000 investment gives you a return of 210% of the appreciated value. In addition, the return on the $160,000 that was not used as part of the purchase price at a 7% return for five years, is equal to $226,000 less the $160,000 for a cash return of $66,000. Combining the $84,000 plus the $66,000 gives you a cash return of $150,000—for a total return of 375%.

The chart in front of me shows on the left, the numbers for someone who used cash to purchase the property, and on the right, the numbers for the person who used leverage to acquire the property: Mr. Allcash earned 80% on his money; Ms. Leverage earned 375%.

Had you used all cash, you would make $84,000 and with leverage only $130,000 ($46,000 more). Your return on investment is significantly higher because of the use of leverage, because of the loan amount.

Now assume that you took the same $40,000 an additional four times and leveraged four different properties. That's how in a five-year period you could take that same block of money, that same $200,000, and at the end of five years you would return $325,000—but in terms of cash and dollars, you've returned that five times, but you still own the real estate. That's how you generate a positive cash flow.

And that's how you still build net worth and equity over time. You use leverage. If you don't use leverage it's almost a waste of time.

Here is a copy of the chart I mentioned earlier.

Capital Appreciation	**Leveraged Transaction**
All Cash	Purchase price: $200,000
Purchase price: $200,000	Cash investment: $40,000
Cash investment: $200,000	Loan amount $160,000

Annual return 7% for five years: Annual return 7% for five years:
$284,000 $284,000
Return on investment: $84,000   Return on investment: $130,000
42% five-year return after cash flow of   210% five-year return of $84,000 plus
$80,000 for a total return of 80%   cash flow of $46,000 for a total
Total cash return: $84,000   return of $325,000
                                          Total cash return: $130,000

Now let's use Total Cost Analysis on the same example given above: $200,000 − 20% down = loan amount $160,000.

It is an investment property so the minimum pay rate on the loan is 1.65%. With that pay rate, the monthly payment is $564. Now if you were going to use a fixed 30-year mortgage, the payment would be 6.625%, which is $1,025 a month. At the end of five years you could refinance the property.

When we talk about refinancing, we talk about the value of the property and the value of the equity.

Let's say the value of the property is $200,000; and the property is appreciating at 6% each year over the next ten years.

So that $200,000 property after ten years is going to be worth $363,879. (A rule of thumb is that money that brings in 7% doubles every 15 years. This seems destined to do even better.)

We have to remember that of the $200,000, $40,000 is the equity portion of the investment.

To arrive at your net profit, you have to subtract $200,000 from the current value of $363,000, leaving you with a profit of $163,000. Dividing $163,000 by $40,000 leaves you a return of investment of 408%.

It is therefore better to buy real estate using leverage than turning to any other investment vehicle where your return is based on the cash investment only.

The Power of Compounding

The theory of compounding is the ability to use the same money over and over again—using that money over and over again to build net worth and to build cash and assets.

In everything we do in real estate, the first thing to look at is the risk. What is the time factor and do we have the best opportunity to return the capital that we invest?

Many people who invested in the stock market are not much better off than they were in earlier days. You have to think carefully about just how much they actually recovered when you read that they had a 24% return on their money from those mutual funds. These people have been told that they had a 24% return on their money. But when did the 24% start?

What no one is telling them is that they were originally down 500%, and yes, they have come back 24%—so now they're being told that they are up 24% for the year. If they calculate it that way, it's a scam. It's a sham. That's not a return on investment, because you haven't got your principal back yet. That's what you have to look at.

STRATEGY #35:
MAKE SURE YOU CAN HANDLE THE RISK.

Risk management is another critical concept in real estate. Usually when people talk about risk, they are talking about losing money, or principal, or capital. One of the biggest risk factors that people don't think about is time.

I hate to tell you this, and this will come as a big surprise to some of you. I don't want to be depressing but we're all going to die. The risk we incur with regard to our investment only occurs while we are alive. I know this sounds silly. Dying is easy. I don't need to get a haircut anymore. I don't need to worry about going to the store anymore. I don't have to worry about anything. It's finished. This may sound harsh. It may even sound unfair to a younger generation who may well feel that the risk incurred is worth it when compared with the importance of taking care of parents, grandparents, etc. So, while it may not be fair to make the younger generation sound heartless, there are certain realities. If you don't think about what happens when your parents and/

or grandparents leave the scene, when it does happen, and your family is not prepared, the consequences could be catastrophic. Whether we like it or not, we have to address these issues that arise for elderly people who need cash flow.

But if I am 89 years old and I don't have any cash, now I am in trouble.

So the bottom line is time. If you have enough time you can deal with this. What happens if you live to 100? What happens is you have to prepare for living that long. We all hope we're going to live at least a little longer than we are right now so that's why you need a plan. It's real simple.

STRATEGY #36:
ANALYZE A PROPERTY BASED ON TIMING.

One of the first things you should look at when analyzing a property is time: are you looking for something in the short term, the intermediate term, or the long term?

I bought properties in 1999 from a client of mine. The market was somewhat depressed at that time, and the properties needed some work. I came to a price with him and we signed a contract to buy these properties for about $142,000 each.

The man I hired to do some of the repair work on them did a great job. We sold the properties off over the next year and a half as the market improved. The client was happy because I put up the money to do the repairs. He made $30,000 on each of the transactions. And I made at least $30,000, sometimes $60,000 on the resale of these properties.

So here we have an example of the function of time. We were able to analyze the marketplace. It wasn't a hot market. I had an instinct to buy these kinds of properties. We had some investors who participated with us, and put up some of the money to make the repairs and they got a good return on their money. We shared in the profits.

STRATEGY #37:
DO YOUR DUE DILIGENCE.

I always recommend that you use an appraiser with whom you develop a relationship—an approved appraiser who will do a fair and honest appraisal. You also need a realtor.

You can't just go to the tax records, because that is not reliable enough. The market is moving in some areas so rapidly that sometimes the tax records are months, or even years behind what's really happening in the market.

You will want to do a review of the cash flow and the expenses involved in the transaction. You must make sure to verify them. It is not unheard of for sellers to lie to realtors and potential buyers. The seller will look you straight in the eye and tell you that this is the greatest property in the world. He will also tell you that he never had a problem with it. Meantime, while you're talking to him, there's a guy coming out on a stretcher who's been shot six times.

So, do your homework. Do some of the due diligence. Do as much as you can. It's worth it. I know from experience—because some people have snookered us. That's why you have to have the right kind of professionals surrounding you. There's always a risk factor.

CHAPTER 16

Mark Mouma: The Handyman Who Buys and Sells Real Estate

I came to Florida in 1989, and I knew I wanted to build wealth. I had been talking to several people who had acquired wealth. Real estate was a good way to do it, they had said.

I was a painting contractor and maintenance man basically taking care of wealthy people in Palm Beach. They too steered me to real estate: "If you want to become wealthy, you have to own real estate." That was the bottom line.

I had put together a few bucks, and I bought my first property in August 1992 just before Hurricane Andrew. I was paying 12% interest. I paid outrageous closing costs, upwards of almost $10,000 for a $40,000 property. I had no idea. I was just happy to get into the game. I had no clue about high or low interest rates, fixed or variable rates. As long as I had found the property that was the best, I felt I was okay. I had a lot to learn. I had a long way to go.

The property was in West Palm Beach. I had one home and I
didn't understand the strategy of holding and refinancing in order
to buy another house. I was under the impression that I needed
to sell the first house in order to get into a second one. When
you're working with minimum funds it's difficult; but I doubled
my money on the house, which at the time seemed like an outstanding feat. But as I look back now, if I had held the property
it would have benefited me much more; I could have rented it.
But that's beside the point. So I bid into another property.

In a nutshell, that blossomed into three properties. Every time
I bought a property I would be broke for months and months. I
would move on to the next one. This is before I learned wealth-
building strategies from the Cutaias. I think I had three properties. I was saving all my money; I had to put down between 20%
and 25% plus closing costs. I was doing it on a shoestring. I was
broke. I had minimum funds. I really struggled those first few
years.

At that particular point, I was young. I would fix properties
up. I'd work all day. I'd work all night. I didn't think anything of
it. In the back of my mind, I knew that later in life I wouldn't be
able to do this by myself. I'd have to hire people. I'm thirty-six
now.

I hit a wall. I found another property. I tried to secure some
financing; but my debt ratio was out of whack. I was paying too
much for these properties even though I was making a little bit of
an income through rental and so forth. The banks have a formula,
and my finances didn't fit. The banks would not extend me any
more credit; I would have to put much more money down. Instead of it becoming easier to obtain property, it was actually becoming harder. As you can imagine, this was very distressing.

At that time I had a dozen or so very wealthy clients who
came here for the winter. I was just the maintenance man to
them—painting, taking the dog to the vet, cleaning out the ga-
rage, watching the house when they were away.

I knew where I wanted to be, and seeing how these people lived increased my motivation. And they gave me a few tips on how to do things. I remember one man in particular who told me, "If you want to become wealthy, you have to talk the talk and walk the walk."

STRATEGY #38:
TALK THE TALK AND WALK THE WALK.

You've got to listen to AM radio. You'll learn the lingo. You'll be able to talk to all the mortgage brokers. Just by understanding a few basic facts your intelligence level will seem higher than it is.

I started listening to AM radio. After a while I kept hearing the Cutaias over and over again. I thought: You know what? I'd like to go down and see what they have to say. This was around 1999 or 2000.

I made an appointment, and brought in my portfolio of properties, closing statements, my expenses, and income reports. Anthony Cutaia's top man laid it all out for me. He was well dressed, very young, energetic. You could tell he knew what was going on.

All my mortgages relied on fixed rates because I didn't know any better. The income was from rentals and quite minimal, just enough to keep the properties alive and make a couple of bucks. (At that point the properties weren't appreciating like they are now.) Cutaia's colleague laid it out for me: "You have to accumulate these properties because down the road they're going to appreciate."

He put it to me this way: How many properties can you afford to have that cost you $50 a month? And how many properties can you afford to have that make you $50 a month? Obviously, you can afford a lot less properties that cost you $50 a month than make you $50 a month.

My main goal at this particular point was the monthly income. My main goal was that I wanted to make $2,500 to $5,000 each month from these properties, basically through rents. I really didn't grasp the fact that they were going to quadruple in value in the early 2000s, and they did.

What the strategies that the Cutaias taught me enabled me to do with these variable rate loans and these interest-only loans and the businessman's loans was to cut my payments in half. That gave me more monthly income, which made my debt ratio flip so on paper I could afford as many properties as I could find. And that's what I did. Having a lower debt ratio also meant that I could get a lower interest rate on my mortgages.

Mortgage lenders don't care how much you owe; they care what you pay. If you owe $20 million and your payment is only $5,000 a month, as opposed to owning $10 million of property, with a $10,000 payment a month, they don't care how much you owe—they only want to know how much of a payment you're responsible for every month (your debt-to-income ratio). I thought my goal was to pay my properties off so I could retire— was I mistaken!

The Cutaias made me realize that I didn't want to pay off my properties—and neither should you! What you want to do is make your monthly income better by lowering your payment. You have more cash flow. If you're paying $1,000 for a property that is bringing in $1,200, you're only making $200; but if your payment goes to $500, you're making $700 a month.

You're not paying off your property. Instead you put the cash into more properties, knowing that down the road they're going to appreciate.

Property is better than the stock market. In a perfect world $10,000 will control a $100,000 property. In stock, $10,000 buys you $10,000 worth of stock. So if that property goes up 10%, you're making 10% on $100,000 and you're leveraging the rest. If your stock goes up 10%, you're only making $1,000. So properties are much better in the long run.

As properties appreciate in value and develop equity, you

should pull that equity out of the property using an interest-only mortgage, keeping your payment reasonable. Look into an option mortgage or a businessman's loan. Don't forget negative amortization. Use all the strategies you've been reading about in this book.

That appointment with the Cutaias' top man changed my life. Here I was with three properties—against the wall because my payments were so high, my monthly income was not that great (according to the people I'm trying to get more loans from), and the income I'm generating from my job and from the properties is not enough to afford more properties.

The Cutaias helped me realize why this was: because of the kind of loans I was getting. Before all I thought was find the right property. It doesn't matter what it takes to get the property, just get it. I didn't realize you could pay $1,000 a month on a normal fixed rate loan. With this other type of loan, the New Smart Loan™, my payments would drop in half. Sometimes less than half, which leaves me able to purchase more properties, which I did. I pulled the money out of these properties and bought more properties.

Some were single-family homes, multiple units. I had two triplexes. I had a couple of condos down on the water. Mostly I bought and held them and then as property values went up I took more money out—I refinanced with the Cutaias on these lower interest loans and took the equity money out and bought more property. I had my 20% down payment from equity of the houses that I owned. Here's how it worked. I would get an appraisal of a property after I had held it for a while and would take it into the Cutaias. I would tell them I wanted to refinance a particular loan based on this new value. Typically you get a 80:20% loan-to-value or a 70:30%, depending on whether it's the primary residence, an income property, a condo—there are a whole bunch of stipulations.

So with a property that has a value of $300,000, I could pull out 70% of that; I'd have a loan of say $250,000 and I only owed $100,000 or $150,000 on the property. They would cut me a check for the difference between what I owed and its new value, which in this case might be $100,000—enough to buy another property or two.

When these new strategies were laid out for me, when I brought my properties in for the first time, it was like somebody threw a switch. I just understood it. And some people never understand it. When I try to explain the strategy to other people who are in similar positions, they just don't understand it. They don't understand: "You mean you don't pay off your property?" I reply: "No, paying off your property's not the goal." They can't grasp that.

The fixed rate strategy and the pay-off-your-house-early strategy—those are all myths that banks, and our parents and grandparents, have taught us, ever since forever. And that's what the bank wants us to do. Make double payments on that mortgage. Pay it down. But you're giving the bank money and then in order to get it back you need to refinance, which means paying the bank more money—or else selling the property.

There is a way to have the money you would have given to the bank available for your use, by using your own coffers, by taking responsibility for your own money and your own actions. You refinance the house, but you don't run off to Europe and buy shoes and watches. It requires discipline. You have to reinvest back into more property. When you really focus on it and look at it, it is borrowed money based on the equity of your properties. You are leveraging your properties in order to get more money so that you can buy more properties.

In a nutshell, I went from $300,000 in properties (which would appreciate at 10 percent a year—$30,000, not bad) to $1.3 million worth of property (appreciating at that same 10 percent— but now $130,000 per year, even better).

Don't get me wrong. It's not a get-rich-quick scheme. This is a get-rich-slow scheme. And it works. It is plain and simple.

Does my yearly income go up? I wouldn't say my yearly income goes up. But my net worth went up tremendously. A lot of it's not liquid. It's wrapped up in properties. Which to some people doesn't really mean wealth, but to me it does. I have an automotive wholesale business. I still have my painting business. I do the rentals. I try to have fun. What I focus on now is how to make money not by what I have to do, but something that's going to bring me a little bit more pleasure, a little bit more enjoyment as I age.

Nine times out of ten the mortgage person or the banker that you are dealing with has no clue about this type of wealth-building process. They just don't grasp it themselves because they've been taught by people who don't know very much either.

This program is for someone who is comfortable using properties to create wealth—you may live in a home for 30 years and create wealth that way.

I've been told I'm building a house of cards, that I'm borrowing money against my property so that I'm going to end up with more debt than I'm going to be able to generate on income, etc. I'm taking all this money and who knows what I'm doing with it and it's all going to implode. People make statements like that because they don't fully understand. You can lead a horse to water, but you can't make him drink.

How hard is it to find property?

It's becoming increasingly harder now that property is appreciating so much here in Palm Beach County. When I started back in 1991 and 1992 property owners were begging you to buy properties off them. I was primarily buying distressed properties because those were the only things I could afford—$30,000, $40,000, $50,000 properties. I had saved up 20% on those and that's what I could afford at the time. I hear people saying, oh if

I had known this at the time, I would have bought all the property I could in Palm Beach County.

That's what I did do. I did buy all the property I could. It wasn't as much as I would have liked to purchase, but it has worked out wonderfully. It's harder to find reasonable property today because you're paying at the high end of the scale for them. You can't find a $300,000 property because it needs a roof, painting, windows. You can't find them for $150,000 either. You're paying top dollar and there are bidding wars out there. The reason: That same property, if you hold on to it for a year, will be worth $350,000 next year. That's $50,000. And you don't have to do anything.

CHAPTER 17

Dan and Gayle Gile: They Began by Helping Dan's Mother-in-Law, and Then Amassed $3 Million in Real Estate Equity

Dan and Gayle Gile came to Florida from New York in 1998 to start a new life. Both had a background in the hair industry and, accordingly they became distributors in that industry. Gayle was born in Brooklyn, New York. Even when she lived in New York she had an interest in real estate. She owned a beauty salon in Brooklyn for 20 years.

Once in Florida, she and her husband rented an apartment for $750 a month for their first year, but they wound up purchasing a home in Lake Worth, Florida, for $164,000.

In 2000, Gayle came across Anthony and Susan Cutaia by listening to the radio as she did every day. She came across the Cutaias' program, "Talk about Mortgages." She was immediately taken with their approach. She decided to give their strategies a try.

STRATEGY #39:
EXPAND YOUR THINKING—USE THESE WEALTH-BUILDING
STRATEGIES TO REACH MORE THAN ONE GOAL.

In the beginning, when the Giles began to realize that it was quite feasible to purchase real estate, they thought only of helping Dan's mother move from Oklahoma to Florida to be closer to them. As Gayle noted: "We did not think of using our real estate for wealth creation. We purchased a condo for her in Delray Beach, two bedrooms and two baths. It cost us $33,000. We took out a $27,000 mortgage, taking some of the equity from the refinance money from the $164,000 home. We paid only $210 a month as a mortgage payment. We had put 20% of the total price down. We learned that if we followed the Cutaias' method, we could create wealth." Again Gale: "I am the type of person. I'll go for it. If I understand it, I'm not afraid. I've been telling relatives: You can do it too. They could have refinanced. But I'm the only one doing it."

One year later the Giles refinanced the condo that they had bought for Dan's mother. At the time it had appreciated to $80,000. Then they took $60,000 in cash from the refinancing to put toward the business that they were setting up.

By this time the Giles were really into buying real estate.

The Giles were also renting a 500-square-foot condo, part of a condo park for which they were paying $600 a month in rent. They decided to purchase their own condo for their distribution business. Dan noticed a sign that went up for a property in Delray Beach, announcing that the Congress Commerce Center, a condo park, was going to be built on the site. That condo became a warehouse and educational center for their beauty business. They were also teaching all phases of the business from the condo.

Dan and Gayle went from the purchase of one property to another.

They took equity from their Delray condo and purchased one of the planned units—each at 3,000 square feet—for $324,000. That was in 2003. That unit, just three years later, is now worth $700,000. While shopping for mortgages at this time, they realized that it wasn't easy to get a small business loan; but they eventually got one through the strategies in this book.

Conscious of the boom that was occurring in south Florida and the fact that builders were building beautiful homes there, the Giles decided to sell their home in Lake Worth, which they had bought for $164,000, and by now had appreciated to $400,000. They found a much larger home in Boynton Beach, for which they paid $400,000. They took the $400,000 that they had acquired by selling the Lake Worth property and put 20% of that sum down in order to buy two condo apartments on the Bay in Latana, Florida. They still had enough left over to buy another condo in Delray Beach for $234,000.

The result of all this buying and selling is that the Giles have close to $3 million in net worth today. They started in 2000 with maybe $100,000. Gayle noted: "We had no real estate assets at that time. I was lucky that the state of Florida made it easy for someone like us to get into real estate. In New York, we would have had to start with $1 million to set up the business, to purchase a home, anything like that. Houses there are $700,000 to start. My $400,000 house is now worth $700,000. We took equity from our Boynton Beach home and bought another condo for $247,000." In the interim Gayle met a neighbor at the first house in Lake Worth. Gayle recalled: "We started talking. She knew everybody from the ground up. She usually tells me what's good in real estate. She gets me to a property before it goes to the public; then I send all the details to my mortgage broker. They tell me if it's a good vehicle. And if it's not worth it, they tell me so. If you can't collect your rent, you don't want to buy it. In certain neighborhoods, the value isn't there, not as much as in other areas."

Gayle and Dan have not been tempted to sell any of their property. They have now acquired enough properties—and have made enough money from these properties—to perhaps buy one large property that will produce enough income for their retirement. Gayle is 54 years old and Dan is 45.

CHAPTER 18

Dean Budney: A New Investor Who Went to Work for the Cutaias

I was born in Schenectady, New York, and raised in nearby Clifton Park. My wife and I currently live in Boca Raton, Florida, and have two children.

In 1999 we had just had our second child. We were living in our first home in Boca Raton. We wanted to find a larger home and so I went to a realtor to help me start looking. On our existing house I had a 30-year fixed mortgage at 7.75% interest. The realtor asked what I planned to do with the present house. Sell it, I suggested, not really realizing there were other, more sensible options.

The realtor suggested I look into the Cutaias and their wealth-building strategies.

I discovered that the biggest debt obligation we put ourselves under is our house. If you can manage your house payments better, you could free up money to spend in other areas. Most people

pour so much of their available cash into monthly mortgage payments that they have nothing left to invest. With the Cutaias'
approach, I had money to redirect into other areas.

It takes 13 years in a standard 30-year fixed mortgage for your
principal to equal your interest payment because the banks stack
the odds in their favor. So you are not really making a dent in
your mortgage for 13 years! But statistics show that people move
on the average of every seven years. Why then take a 15-year or
30-year mortgage?

STRATEGY #40:
DON'T SELL PROPERTIES; TURN THEM INTO INVESTMENT
PROPERTIES.

Using what I had learned, I decided to keep our existing home
and refinance it, convert it to an investment property, and then
purchase the new home.

Of course I was planning to have a mortgage on the new
house I was purchasing and I didn't think I could carry two mortgages at the same time. But I could once I looked at my financing
differently.

I decided on an option ARM mortgage. Its most unique feature was that it had four monthly payment options. I had a choice
every month as to how much I wanted to pay the lender.

The first option was the minimum-payment one; the second,
interest-only; the third was as if I were amortizing the loan over
15 years; and the fourth, as if I were amortizing over 30 years.

The minimum-payment option looked very attractive. I would
lower my payment on a monthly basis considerably while at the
same time I would get cash back since my existing house had
appreciated in value and I could draw cash out of that property.

I think we took $15,000 or $20,000 out of the equity in the
original house. We used that cash as part of our down payment
and to cover the closing costs on the new house.

If I had not chosen the option ARM mortgage with the low minimum payment, I would not have been able to rent it out with a positive cash flow. With the 30-year fixed mortgage on the existing house, there would have been a negative $300 a month cash flow. Now I had a positive cash flow of $400 a month.

My initial thought after hearing about these mortgage instruments was, "How come I never heard about this mortgage before?" It had been around for a few years. All that I knew about in the past was that you had two choices when it came to mortgages, the 15-year fixed mortgage or the 30-year fixed mortgage. Is the option ARM mortgage really available through major institutional lenders? Absolutely.

I realized that the option ARM was truly advantageous to the consumer because it gave the consumer such great flexibility. You decide each and every month how much money you will pay into your mortgage. I liked that. The payment creates a positive cash flow. Thus we actually could use the same mortgage to purchase the new house. It took us a couple of months. But by then I had already refinanced the house I was in. And so I was able to use the same kind of mortgage for the new house.

There is a risk that interest rates will climb. But there is some protection built into the option ARM program against a rise in interest rates. It is the annual payment cap. That sold me on the option ARM program. The monthly payment cannot go up more than 7.5% of the payment in any given year. So if the payment were $1,000 a month, no matter what the interest rates were, the payment could not go up more than $75 a month in a given year. The payment cap would stay in place for five years. So you could be assured that your payment would only change within those parameters.

I had the best of both worlds. It was truly a win-win situation: I lowered my monthly mortgage payment. That created a positive cash flow for my original house, which I was renting out. This positive cash flow, in turn, permitted me to take cash from the equity in the existing house to use toward the purchase of the new house. I did not have to come up with so much money to put down on the new house. So it was just a clear win all the way around.

After three years in the new home I refinanced it and I followed the Cutaias' recommendation to draw equity out of the house and redirect that money to either a new property or into some other investment vehicle that gave me a compound rate of return.

At this time I finally accepted Anthony Cutaia's long-standing offer that I come work for him. He had been asking me to come on board for the past three years. He kept telling me I ought to consider his offer seriously. After all, he would say, you have followed the exact philosophy we talk about; and you are a living example of what we tell clients to do.

And so in July 2003, I began working for Anthony. I am about to celebrate my third anniversary of working for him.

Our approach at Cutaia Mortgage was totally different from anything I had heard about before. It was very refreshing to know that an alternative existed out there. The only thing my parents and their generation had heard was: pay off the mortgage as quickly as possible. I no longer think that way—and neither will my children!

Strategies

Here are the forty strategies listed in the order they appear in the book:

STRATEGY #1: CONVERT THE "DEAD MONEY" YOU HAVE IN HOME EQUITY INTO USABLE CASH.

STRATEGY #2: USE LEVERAGE TO CREATE WEALTH.

STRATEGY #3: KEEP YOUR MONEY OUT OF THE BANK'S HANDS. NEVER PAY OFF YOUR MORT-GAGE—NEVER!

STRATEGY #4: FIND A MORTGAGE FIRST, THEN FIND THE PROPERTY.

STRATEGY #5: STOP THINKING THAT BEING DEBT FREE IS GOOD.

STRATEGY #6: LET THE MONTHLY MORTGAGE PAY-

MENT DETERMINE YOUR CHOICE OF MORTGAGE, NOT INTEREST RATES.

STRATEGY #7: DEVELOP CLEAR-CUT OBJECTIVES FOR USING THE CASH YOU WILL DRAW OUT OF YOUR PROPERTY.

STRATEGY #8: LET YOUR PROPERTY APPRECIATE IN VALUE; THEN EXTRACT (HARVEST) THE CASH FROM IT.

STRATEGY #9: WITH THE CASH YOU SAVE BY PAYING A LOWER MONTHLY MORTGAGE PAYMENT, LOOK FOR WEALTH-CREATION STRATEGIES THROUGH REAL ESTATE VENTURES.

STRATEGY #10: MAKE MINIMUM MONTHLY MORTGAGE PAYMENTS AND NEVER MAKE EXTRA PAYMENTS.

STRATEGY #11: LEARN AS MUCH AS YOU CAN ABOUT MORTGAGE PROGRAMS. IF YOU DON'T, YOU WILL PAY A HEAVY PRICE FOR NOT DOING YOUR RESEARCH.

STRATEGY #12: USE LEVERAGE TO CREATE "GOOD" DEBT.

STRATEGY #13: BE DISCIPLINED WITH YOUR NEW USABLE CASH; DON'T FRITTER IT AWAY ON BOATS AND VACATIONS.

STRATEGY #14: EXPLOIT THE FLEXIBILITY OF NEW SMART LOANS™ BY VARYING YOUR MORTGAGE PAYMENTS FROM MONTH TO MONTH.

STRATEGY #15: INVEST YOUR NEW "USABLE" CASH IN COMPOUND ACCOUNTS—THAT'S HOW TO BUILD WEALTH.

STRATEGY #16: NEVER PAY OFF THE PRINCIPAL IN YOUR MORTGAGE.

STRATEGY #17: CHOOSE AN INTEREST-ONLY LOAN, AND HAVE THE ABILITY TO PAY OFF YOUR MORTGAGE FASTER THAN WITH A MORE CONVENTIONAL LOAN.

STRATEGY #18: IF YOU PLAN TO LIVE IN YOUR HOME FOR ONLY A BRIEF AMOUNT OF TIME OR LONGER, CHOOSE AN INTEREST-ONLY MORTGAGE.

STRATEGY #19: TO PURCHASE A LARGER HOME WITH A LOWER MONTHLY MORTGAGE PAYMENT, CHOOSE A NEGATIVE AMORTIZATION MORTGAGE.

STRATEGY #20: IF YOU KNOW THAT YOUR INCOME WILL INCREASE DRAMATICALLY IN THE NEAR FUTURE, CHOOSE THE "NEGAM" MORTGAGE OPTION.

STRATEGY #21: SELECT A NEGAM MORTGAGE IF YOU WANT TO INCREASE YOUR CASH FLOW IN THE SHORT RUN.

STRATEGY #22: USE TENANTS IN COMMON AGREEMENT IN ORDER TO MAKE IT EASIER TO USE 1031 EXCHANGES AND COST SEGREGATION ANALYSES.

STRATEGY #23: USE TENANTS IN COMMON OPTION TO GET TAX-SHELTERED CASH FLOW.

STRATEGY #24: USE A 1031 EXCHANGE AND AVOID PAYING CAPITAL GAINS WHEN SELLING PROPERTIES.

STRATEGY #25: SELECT A 1031 EXCHANGE TO ACQUIRE A MORE VALUABLE PIECE OF REAL ESTATE THAN THE ONE BEING SOLD.

STRATEGY #26: BE AN INVESTOR, NOT A DEALER.

STRATEGY #27: USE THESE STRATEGIES ON MULTIPLE PROPERTIES.

STRATEGY #28: TO SHELTER LARGE AMOUNTS OF

MONEY FROM TAX LIABILITY, ENGAGE IN A COST SEGREGATION STUDY.

STRATEGY #29: TO DEFER THE MAXIMUM AMOUNT OF INCOME TAX, COMBINE COST SEGREGATION ANALYSIS WITH A 1031 EXCHANGE.

STRATEGY #30: MAINTAIN FOCUS.

STRATEGY #31: AVOID BECOMING A JUMPER.

STRATEGY #32: SURROUND YOURSELF WITH PEOPLE WHO ARE SMARTER THAN YOU ARE.

STRATEGY #33: DON'T BE CHEAP.

STRATEGY #34: DON'T BE AFRAID OF LITIGATION.

STRATEGY #35: MAKE SURE YOU CAN HANDLE THE RISK.

STRATEGY #36: ANALYZE A PROPERTY BASED ON TIMING.

STRATEGY #37: DO YOUR DUE DILIGENCE.

STRATEGY #38: TALK THE TALK AND WALK THE WALK.

STRATEGY #39: EXPAND YOUR THINKING—USE THESE WEALTH-BUILDING STRATEGIES TO REACH MORE THAN ONE GOAL.

STRATEGY #40: DON'T SELL PROPERTIES; TURN THEM INTO INVESTMENT PROPERTIES.

Total Cost Analysis Charts and Graphs

The following graphics were generated using
The Mortgage Coach Software. For more information,
please go to www.mortgagecoach.com.

Total Cost Analysis Bar Chart I
NEW BORROWER
ANYWERE USA

FOLLOW THESE 3 SIMPLE STEPS:

1. The purpose of this analysis is to provide you with a visual report of the Total Cost Analysis.

2. Compare the graphs in each program and isolate the Principal and Interest amounts for each program.

3. Call your loan representative to obtain further information.

> The purpose of this bar chart analysis is to help you make an informed decision.

New Smart Loan

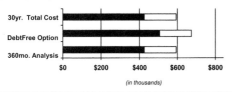

(in thousands)

	Interest	Principal	Total
30yr. Total Cost	$427,282	$166,670	**$593,952**
DebtFree Option	$507,682	$280,000	**$787,682**
360mo. Analysis	$507,682	$280,000	**$787,682**

---

30 Fix 0 Pts

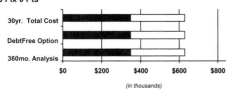

(in thousands)

	Interest	Principal	Total
30yr. Total Cost	$348,861	$280,000	**$628,861**
DebtFree Option	$348,861	$280,000	**$628,861**
360mo. Analysis	$348,861	$280,000	**$628,861**

---

5 Yr I/O 1 Pt

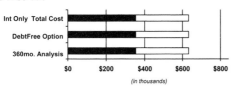

(in thousands)

	Interest	Principal	Total
Int Only Total Cost	$352,100	$280,000	**$632,100**
DebtFree Option	$352,100	$280,000	**$632,100**
360mo. Analysis	$352,100	$280,000	**$632,100**

(continues)

5 Yr I/O 0 Pt

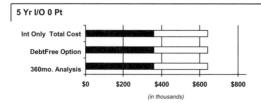

(in thousands)

	Interest	Principal	Total
Int Only Total Co	$360,850	$280,000	$640,850
DebtFree Option	$360,850	$280,000	$640,850
360mo. Analysis	$360,850	$280,000	$640,850

Total Cost Analysis Bar Chart II
NEW BORROWER
ANYWERE USA

FOLLOW THESE 3 SIMPLE STEPS:

1. The purpose of this analysis is to provide you with a visual report of the Total Cost Analysis.

2. Compare the graphs in each program and isolate the Principal and Interest amounts for each program.

3. Call your loan representative to obtain further information.

The purpose of this bar chart analysis is to help you make an informed decision.

New Smart Loan

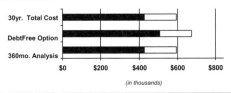

(in thousands)

	Interest	Principal	Total
30yr. Total Cost	$427,282	$166,670	**$593,952**
DebtFree Option	$507,682	$280,000	**$787,682**
360mo. Analysis	$507,682	$280,000	**$787,682**

30 Fix 0 Pts

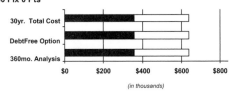

(in thousands)

	Interest	Principal	Total
30yr. Total Cost	$357,125	$280,000	**$637,125**
DebtFree Option	$357,125	$280,000	**$637,125**
360mo. Analysis	$357,125	$280,000	**$637,125**

15 YR FIXED

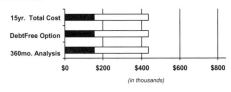

(in thousands)

	Interest	Principal	Total
15yr. Total Cost	$155,582	$280,000	**$435,582**
Debtfree Option	$155,582	$280,000	**$435,582**
360mo. Analysis	$155,582	$280,000	**$435,582**

(continues)

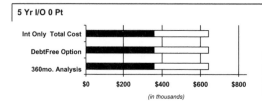

5 Yr I/O 0 Pt

	Interest	Principal	Total
Int Only Total Co	$360,850	$280,000	**$640,850**
DebtFree Option	$360,850	$280,000	**$640,850**
360mo. Analysis	$360,850	$280,000	**$640,850**

> The purpose of this analysis is to help you make an informed decision when selecting your home loan.

Total Cost Analysis I

NEW BORROWER
ANYWERE USA

FOLLOW THESE 3 SIMPLE STEPS:
1. Review the SUMMARY of your loans. Details for each program can be found on the second page.
2. Next, review the TOTAL COST ANALYSIS for each loan so that you can compare which program might be right for your financial situation.*
3. Finally, review the suggested Debt Free or Asset Accum. plan to see how you can save thousands on your loan. Also, you can review the MONTHLY TAX BENEFITS.

SUMMARY

This summary table displays information on up to four loan programs, including their respective fees and monthly payments.

Each program shows a first mortgage, and possibly a second mortgage.

Although this table will show you which loan will provide you the lowest payment, such a loan may not be the right loan for your financial situation.*

		New Smart Loan	30 Fix 0 Pts	5 Yr I/O 1 Pt	5 Yr I/O 0 Pt
1st	Loan Amount	$280,000	$280,000	$280,000	$280,000
	Interest Rate	1.000%	6.375%	5.250%	5.875%
	Term (months)	360	360	Int. Only	Int. Only
	P&I	$901	$1,747	$1,225	$1,371
	MI	$0	$0	$0	$0
	MI Cut Off	N/A	N/A	N/A	N/A
2nd	Loan Amount	$0	$0	$0	$0
	Interest Rate	0.000%	0.000%	0.000%	0.000%
	Term (months)	180	180	180	180
	P&I	$0	$0	$0	$0
Totals	Total Payment	$901	$1,747	$1,225	$1,371
	Net Savings	$846	$0	$522	$376

TOTAL COST ANALYSIS

A true loan comparison cannot be made simply by comparing the payments that a loan offers. There are various other fees and issues which effect the overall cost of a loan. The table at the right analyzes the difference in total overall cost of your home loan.

Evaluating the total cost is the key to selecting the lowest cost mortgage for your individual needs.*

Months: 360	New Smart Loan	30 Fix 0 Pts	5 Yr I/O 1 Pt	5 Yr I/O 0 Pt
Total Payment	$787,682	$628,861	$632,100	$640,850
Principal Paid	$280,000	$280,000	$280,000	$280,000
Int / MI Paid	$507,682	$348,861	$352,100	$360,850
Balance Left	$0	$0	$0	$0
Closing & Pts.	$5,900	$3,100	$5,900	$3,100
Total Cost	$513,582	$351,961	$358,000	$363,950
Net Savings	$0	$161,621	$155,582	$149,632

MORTGAGE PLAN WITH ASSET ACCUMULATION

This Mortgage Plan is designed to help you make an informed decision on a mortgage integrated with your overall financial plan. This example displays an estimated Real Estate value combined with potential investment account growth.*

	New Smart Loan	30 Fix 0 Pts	5 Yr I/O 1 Pt	5 Yr I/O 0 Pt
Monthly Amount	$846	$0	$522	$376
Int. Rate	6.00%	0.00%	6.00%	6.00%
Home Value	$446,699	$446,699	$446,699	$446,699
Loan Balance	$300,301	$261,731	$280,000	$280,000
Equity	$146,397	$184,968	$166,699	$166,699
Accum. Total	$30,546	$0	$37,124	$26,741
Net Worth	$176,944	$184,968	$203,823	$193,439
Home Value	$570,113	$570,113	$570,113	$570,113
Loan Balance	$276,877	$236,624	$280,000	$280,000
Equity	$293,236	$333,489	$290,113	$290,113
Accum. Total	$41,202	$0	$107,170	$93,153
Net Worth	$334,438	$333,489	$397,283	$383,266
Assets > Debts	26.42 yrs.	30.00 yrs.	18.25 yrs.	19.17 yrs.

Years: 5 .... >

Years: 10 .... >

(continues)

MONTHLY TAX BENEFIT

Consider the tax benefits of your home mortgage. By consolidating your non-tax deductible debt (credit cards, etc.) into your mortgage, you can save $$$. This is just an estimate - contact your tax consultant for advice.

Tax Brac: 33%	New Smart Loan	30 Fix 0 Pts	5 Yr I/O 1 Pt	5 Yr I/O 0 Pt
1st Mortgage	$609	$491	$404	$452
2nd Mortgage	$0	$0	$0	$0
Property Tax	$0	$0	$0	$0
Total Monthly	$609	$491	$404	$452
Net Savings	$205	$87	$0	$48

DETAIL

The Detail table below discloses the financial information used to calculate the tables above. For further information, speak with your professional mortgage advisor.*

	New Smart Loan		30 Fix 0 Pts		5 Yr I/O 1 Pt		5 Yr I/O 0 Pt	
Value	$350,000		$350,000		$350,000		$350,000	
Equity (%)	20.000%	0.000%	20.000%	0.000%	20.000%	0.000%	20.000%	0.000%
	1st Mtg.	2nd Mtg.	1st Mtg.	2nd Mtg.	1st Mtg.	2nd Mtg.	1st Mtg.	2nd Mtg.
Loan Amount	$280,000	$0	$280,000	$0	$280,000	$0	$280,000	$0
Loan Type	NegAm	"HELOC"	Fixed	"HELOC"	Adjustable	"HELOC"	Adjustable	"HELOC"
Interest Rate	1.000%	0.000%	6.375%	0.000%	5.250%	0.000%	5.875%	0.000%
Term	360	180	360	180	Int. Only	180	Int. Only	180
Closing	$3,100	$0	$3,100	$0	$3,100	$0	$3,100	$0
Points	1.000%	0.000%	0.000%	0.000%	1.000%	0.000%	0.000%	0.000%
APR	8.133%	0.000%	6.480%	0.000%	4.282%	0.000%	4.345%	0.000%
Principal & Int.	$901	$0	$1,747	$0	$1,225	$0	$1,371	$0
Mtg. Ins.	$0		$0		$0		$0	
Total P&I	$901		$1,747		$1,225		$1,371	
Index	MTA				1yr Tres		1yr Tres	
Margin	3.500%				2.750%		2.750%	
LifeCap	9.950%				10.250%		10.875%	
Scenario	1				1		1	
First Adj Cap					2.000%		2.000%	
First Adj Mos	2				61		61	
Adj Cap					2.000%		2.000%	
Adj Mos					12		12	
HOA	$0		$0		$0		$0	
Haz Ins.	$0		$0		$0		$0	
Prop Taxes	$0		$0		$0		$0	
Other	$0		$0		$0		$0	
Pymt. Adjust.								
Adj Cap%	7.500%							
Adj Per (Mos)	12							
Recast Pd/Stop	60 / 60							
Max Balance	110%							
PITI	$901	$0	$1,747	$0	$1,225	$0	$1,371	$0
Term Reduction	$0	$0	$0	$0	$0	$0	$0	$0
Total PITI	$901		$1,747		$1,225		$1,371	
Mo. Asset A.	$846		$0		$522		$376	
Asset A. IntRate	6.000%		0.000%		6.000%		6.000%	
Asset A. Open	$0		$0		$522		$376	

NOTES

Trusted Advisor

> The purpose of this analysis is to help you make an informed decision when selecting your home loan.

Total Cost Analysis II

NEW BORROWER
ANYWERE USA

FOLLOW THESE 3 SIMPLE STEPS:
1. Review the SUMMARY of your loans. Details for each program can be found on the second page.
2. Next, review the TOTAL COST ANALYSIS for each loan so that you can compare which program might be right for your financial situation.*
3. Finally, review the suggested Debt Free or Asset Accum. plan to see how you can save thousands on your loan. Also, you can review the MONTHLY TAX BENEFITS.

SUMMARY

This summary table displays information on up to four loan programs, including their respective fees and monthly payments.

Each program shows a first mortgage, and possibly a second mortgage.

Although this table will show you which loan will provide you the lowest payment, such a loan may not be the right loan for your financial situation.*

		New Smart Loan	30 Fix 0 Pts	15 YR FIXED	5 Yr I/O 0 Pt
1st	Loan Amount	$280,000	$280,000	$280,000	$280,000
	Interest Rate	1.000%	6.500%	6.375%	5.875%
	Term (months)	360	360	180	Int. Only
	P&I	$901	$1,770	$2,420	$1,371
	MI	$0	$0	$0	$0
	MI Cut Off	N/A	N/A	N/A	N/A
2nd	Loan Amount	$0	$0	$0	$0
	Interest Rate	0.000%	0.000%	0.000%	0.000%
	Term (months)	180	180	180	180
	P&I	$0	$0	$0	$0
Totals	Total Payment	$901	$1,770	$2,420	$1,371
	Net Savings	$1,519	$650	$0	$1,049

TOTAL COST ANALYSIS

A true loan comparison cannot be made simply by comparing the payments that a loan offers. There are various other fees and issues which effect the overall cost of a loan. The table at the right analyzes the difference in total overall cost of your home loan.

Evaluating the total cost is the key to selecting the lowest cost mortgage for your individual needs.*

Months: 360	New Smart Loan	30 Fix 0 Pts	15 YR FIXED	5 Yr I/O 0 Pt
Total Payment	$787,682	$637,125	$435,582	$640,850
Principal Paid	$280,000	$280,000	$280,000	$280,000
Int / MI Paid	$507,682	$357,125	$155,582	$360,850
Balance Left	$0	$0	$0	$0
Closing & Pts.	$5,900	$3,100	$3,100	$3,100
Total Cost	$513,582	$360,225	$158,682	$363,950
Net Savings	$0	$153,357	$354,899	$149,632

MORTGAGE PLAN WITH ASSET ACCUMULATION

This Mortgage Plan is designed to help you make an informed decision on a mortgage integrated with your overall financial plan. This example displays an estimated Real Estate value combined with potential investment account growth.*

	New Smart Loan	30 Fix 0 Pts	15 YR FIXED	5 Yr I/O 0 Pt
Monthly Amount	$1,500	$0	$0	$376
Int. Rate	6.00%	0.00%	0.00%	6.00%
Home Value	$570,113	$570,113	$570,113	$570,113
Loan Balance	$276,877	$237,373	$124,049	$280,000
Equity	$293,236	$332,740	$446,064	$290,113
Years: 10				
Accum. Total	$271,307	$0	$0	$93,153
Net Worth	**$564,543**	**$332,740**	**$446,064**	**$383,266**
Home Value	$727,625	$727,625	$727,625	$727,625
Loan Balance	$242,100	$203,166	$0	$280,000
Equity	$485,524	$524,459	$727,625	$447,625
Years: 15				
Accum. Total	$395,312	$0	$0	$182,733
Net Worth	**$880,836**	**$524,459**	**$727,625**	**$630,357**
Assets > Debts	10.33 yrs.	30.00 yrs.	15.00 yrs.	19.17 yrs.

(continues)

MONTHLY TAX BENEFIT

Consider the tax benefits of your home mortgage. By consolidating your non-tax deductible debt (credit cards, etc.) into your mortgage, you can save $$$. This is just an estimate - contact your tax consultant for advice.

Tax Brac: 33%	New Smart Loan	30 Fix 0 Pts	15 YR FIXED	5 Yr I/O 0 Pt
1st Mortgage	$609	$501	$491	$452
2nd Mortgage	$0	$0	$0	$0
Property Tax	$0	$0	$0	$0
Total Monthly	$609	$501	$491	$452
Net Savings	$157	$48	$39	$0

DETAIL

The Detail table below discloses the financial information used to calculate the tables above. For further information, speak with your professional mortgage advisor.*

	New Smart Loan		30 Fix 0 Pts		15 YR FIXED		5 Yr I/O 0 Pt	
Value	$350,000		$350,000		$350,000		$350,000	
Equity (%)	20.000%	0.000%	20.000%	0.000%	20.000%	0.000%	20.000%	0.000%
	1st Mtg.	2nd Mtg.	1st Mtg.	2nd Mtg.	1st Mtg.	2nd Mtg.	1st Mtg.	2nd Mtg.
Loan Amount	$280,000	$0	$280,000	$0	$280,000	$0	$280,000	$0
Loan Type	NegAm	"HELOC"	Fixed	"HELOC"	Fixed	"HELOC"	Adjustable	"HELOC"
Interest Rate	1.000%	0.000%	6.500%	0.000%	6.375%	0.000%	5.875%	0.000%
Term	360	180	360	180	180	180	Int. Only	180
Closing	$3,100	$0	$3,100	$0	$3,100	$0	$3,100	$0
Points	1.000%	0.000%	0.000%	0.000%	0.000%	0.000%	0.000%	0.000%
APR	8.133%	0.000%	6.607%	0.000%	6.551%	0.000%	4.345%	0.000%
Principal & Int.	$901	$0	$1,770	$0	$2,420	$0	$1,371	$0
Mtg. Ins.	$0		$0		$0		$0	
Total P&I	**$901**		**$1,770**		**$2,420**		**$1,371**	
Index	MTA						1yr Tres	
Margin	3.500%						2.750%	
LifeCap	9.950%						10.875%	
Scenario	1						1	
First Adj Cap							2.000%	
First Adj Mos	2						61	
Adj Cap							2.000%	
Adj Mos							12	
HOA	$0		$0		$0		$0	
Haz Ins.	$0		$0		$0		$0	
Prop Taxes	$0		$0		$0		$0	
Other	$0		$0		$0		$0	
Pymt. Adjust.								
Adj Cap%	7.500%							
Adj Per (Mos)	12							
Recast Pd/Stop	60 / 60							
Max Balance	110%							
PITI	$901	$0	$1,770	$0	$2,420	$0	$1,371	$0
Term Reduction	$0	$0	$0	$0	$0	$0	$0	$0
Total PITI	**$901**		**$1,770**		**$2,420**		**$1,371**	
Mo. Asset A.	$1,500		$0		$0		$376	
Asset A. IntRate	6.000%		0.000%		0.000%		6.000%	
Asset A. Open	$96,000		$0		$0		$376	

NOTES

Trusted Advisor

Total Cost Analysis Graphs
NEW BORROWER
ANYWERE USA

. . . .

The purpose of this analysis is to help you make an
informed decision when comparing programs and
making prepayments on your mortgage.

BEFORE PREPAYMENT

*The graphs at the right show you
principal and interest over time. The
point where you build equity is
where the upward sloping principal
amount crosses the downward
sloping interest amount.*

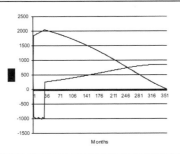

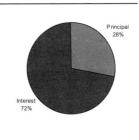

Principal
28%

Interest
72%

AFTER PREPAYMENT

*The graphs at the right show you
principal and interest over time.
Notice that the equity point has
moved eariler in time. This
indicates that you are building
equity quicker when you prepay
into your mortgage.*

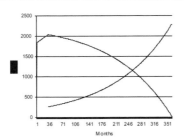

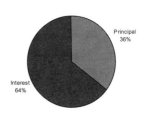

Principal
36%

Interest
64%

INTEREST SAVINGS

*Interest savings based on our
proposed periodic prepayment
amount.*

Prepay $1,500	Interest	Principal
Before prepayment	$427,282	$166,670
After prepayment	$507,682	$280,000
Interest Savings:	($80,400)	
Debt Free in x years:	.0	

FOLLOW THESE 3 SIMPLE STEPS:

1 SUMMARY displays a comparison showing your total monthly rent vs a breakdown of a proposed mortgage plan

2. Review and compare the benefits of homeownership over time

3. ASSET ACCUMULATION shows how you can invest x amount of money for your future to increase your net worth

Rent vs. Own

NEW BORROWER

ANYWERE USA

Summary

This summary table displays the benefit opportunity of homeownership. The rent column displays the amount you are currently paying in rent. The buy column reflects the cost and benefits of homeownership.

See the benefits of Homeownership in action. After taxes, your net monthly cost of Homeownership would be: **$997**

Offering a monthly Homeowner benefit of: **$528**

Rent		Homeownership	
Rent	$1,500	P&I	$1,365
Insurance/Other	$25	Taxes/Insurance/HOA	$315
Total Rent	**$1,525**	**Total PITI**	**$1,681**
		Tax Benefits	$464
		Principal Paid	$219
Net Monthly Cost	**$1,525**	**Net Monthly Cost**	**$997**

Assumptions		Assumptions	
Rental Increase/Yr	3%	Appreciation	3%
		Tax Bracket	33%
		Purchase Price	$250,000
		Interest Rate	6.125%
		APR	6.336%
		Down Payment	$25,000
		Closing Costs	$5,100
		Total Cash to Close	$30,100

Ownership Analysis

The benefits of Homeownership can be seen over time. The tables in this analysis reflect the cost savings as well as the equity you will build based on principle reduction and appreciation rates of your property.

Months: 120

Rent		Homeownership	
Total Payment	$209,350	Total PITI	$201,663
Principal Paid	$0	Principal Paid	$36,152
Tax Benefit	$0	Tax Benefit	$52,441
Net Cost	**$209,350**	**Net Cost**	**$113,071**
Real Estate Value	$0	Real Estate Value	$335,979
Loan Balance	$0	Loan Balance	$188,848
Total Home Equity	**$0**	**Total Home Equity**	**$147,131**

Months: 360

Rent		Homeownership	
Total Payment	$865,357	Total PITI	$604,989
Principal Paid	$0	Principal Paid	$223,642
Tax Benefit	$0	Tax Benefit	$119,238
Net Cost	**$865,357**	**Net Cost**	**$262,109**
Real Estate Value	$0	Real Estate Value	$606,816
Loan Balance	$0	Loan Balance	$1,358
Total Home Equity	**$0**	**Total Home Equity**	**$605,457**

(continues)

Asset Accumulation

The benefits displayed in asset accumulation show how investing monthly can increase your net worth.

Investment		Investment	
Opening Balance	$30,000	Opening Balance	$464
Monthly Amount	$0	Monthly Amount	$464
Return Avg.	8.000%	Return Avg.	8.000%
Years	**Amount**	**Years**	**Amount**
10 yrs	$66,589	10 yrs	$85,917
30 yrs	$328,072	30 yrs	$696,601
Benefits		**Benefits**	
By 30 yrs, your TOTAL NET WORTH will reach $328,072.		By 30 yrs, your home's equity is $605,457. Your asset account is $696,601. Your TOTAL NET WORTH will reach $1,302,058.	

Glossary

acceleration clause
Provision in a mortgage that allows the lender to demand payment of the entire principal balance if a monthly payment is missed or some other default occurs.

additional principal payment
Way to reduce the remaining balance on the loan by paying more than the scheduled principal amount due.

adjustable rate mortgage (ARM)
Mortgage with an interest rate that changes during the life of the loan according to movements in an index rate. Sometimes called AMLs (adjustable mortgage loans) or VRMs (variable-rate mortgages).

adjusted basis
Cost of a property plus the value of any capital expenditures for improvements to the property minus any depreciation taken.

adjustment date
Date that the interest rate changes on an adjustable rate mortgage (ARM).

adjustment period
Period elapsing between adjustment dates for an adjustable rate mortgage (ARM).

affordability analysis
Analysis of a buyer's ability to afford the purchase of a home. It reviews income, liabilities, and available funds, and considers the type of mortgage you plan to use, the area where you want to purchase a home, and the closing costs that are likely.

amortization
Gradual repayment of a mortgage loan, both principal and interest, by installments.

amortization term
Length of time required to amortize the mortgage loan expressed as a number of months. For example, 360 months is the amortization term for a 30-year fixed rate mortgage.

annual percentage rate (APR)
Cost of credit, expressed as a yearly rate including interest, mortgage insurance, and loan origination fees. This allows the buyer to compare loans; however, APR should not be confused with the actual note rate.

appraisal
Written analysis prepared by a qualified appraiser that estimates the value of a property.

appraised value
Opinion of a property's fair market value, based on an appraiser's knowledge, experience, and analysis of the property.

asset
Anything owned of monetary value including real property, personal property, and enforceable claims against others (including bank accounts, stocks, mutual funds, etc.).

assignment
Transfer of a mortgage from one person to another.

assumability
Ability of a mortgage to be transferred from the seller to the new buyer. Generally requires a credit review of the new borrower, and lenders may charge a fee for the assumption. If a mortgage contains a due-on-sale clause, a new buyer may not assume it.

assumption fee
Fee paid to a lender (usually by the purchaser of real property) when an assumption takes place.

balance sheet
Financial statement that shows assets, liabilities, and net worth as of a specific date.

balloon mortgage
Mortgage with level monthly payments that amortizes over a stated term but also requires that a lump sum payment be paid at the end of a previously specified term.

balloon payment
Final lump sum paid at the maturity date of a balloon mortgage.

before-tax income
Income before taxes are deducted.

biweekly payment mortgage
Plan to reduce the debt every two weeks (instead of the standard monthly payment schedule). The 26 (or possibly 27) biweekly

payments are each equal to one-half of the monthly payment required if the loan were a standard 30-year fixed rate mortgage. The result for the borrower is a substantial savings in interest.

bridge loan
Second mortgage, collateralized by the borrower's present home, that allows the proceeds to be used to close on a new house before the present home is sold. Also known as a "swing loan."

broker
Individual or company that brings borrowers and lenders together for the purpose of loan origination.

buy-down
When the seller, builder, or buyer pays an amount of money up front to the lender to reduce monthly payments during the first few years of a mortgage. Buy-downs can occur in both fixed and adjustable rate mortgages.

2/1 buy-down mortgage
The 2/1 buy-down mortgage allows the borrower to qualify at below market rates so they can borrow more. The initial starting interest rate increases by 1% at the end of the first year and adjusts again by another 1% at the end of the second year. It then remains at a fixed interest rate for the remainder of the loan term. Borrowers often refinance at the end of the second year to obtain the best long-term rates; however, even keeping the loan in place for three full years or more will keep their average interest rate in line with the original market conditions.

cap
Limits how much the interest rate or the monthly payment can increase, either at each adjustment or during the life of the mort-

gage. Payment caps don't limit the amount of interest the lender is earning and may cause negative amortization.

Certificate of Eligibility
Document issued by the federal government certifying a veteran's eligibility for a Department of Veterans Affairs (VA) mortgage.

Certificate of Reasonable Value (CRV)
Document issued by the Department of Veterans Affairs (VA) that establishes the maximum value and loan amount for a VA mortgage.

change frequency
The frequency (in months) of payment and/or interest rate changes in an adjustable rate mortgage (ARM).

closing
Meeting held to finalize the sale of a property. The buyer signs the mortgage documents and pays closing costs. Also called "settlement."

closing costs
Expenses—over and above the price of the property—that are incurred by buyers and sellers when transferring ownership of a property. Closing costs normally include an origination fee, property taxes, charges for title insurance and escrow costs, appraisal fees, etc. Closing costs will vary according to the area, country, and the lenders used, but are not insignificant, averaging about 3 to 5% of the amount of the loan.

compound interest
Interest paid on the original principal balance and on the accrued and unpaid interest.

consumer reporting agency/bureau
An organization that handles the preparation of reports used by lenders to determine a potential borrower's credit history. The agency/bureau gets data for these reports from a credit repository and from other sources.

conversion clause
Provision in an ARM allowing the loan to be converted to a fixed rate mortgage at some point during the term. Usually conversion is allowed at the end of the first adjustment period. The conversion feature may cost extra.

credit report
Report detailing an individual's credit history that is prepared by a credit bureau and used by a lender to determine a loan applicant's creditworthiness.

credit risk score
Measures a consumer's credit risk relative to the rest of the U.S. population, based on the individual's credit usage history. The credit score most widely used by lenders is the FICO® score, developed by Fair, Issac and Company. This three-digit number, ranging from 300 to 850, is calculated by a mathematical equation that evaluates many types of information that are on your credit report. Higher FICO® scores represent lower credit risks, which typically equate to better loan terms. In general, credit scores are critical in the mortgage loan underwriting process. Also called "credit score."

deed of trust
Document used in some states instead of a mortgage. Title is conveyed to a trustee.

default
Failure to make mortgage payments on a timely basis or to comply with other requirements of a mortgage.

delinquency
Failure to make mortgage payments on time.

deposit
Sum of money given to bind the sale of real estate, or a sum of money given to ensure payment or an advance of funds in the processing of a loan.

discount
In an ARM with an initial rate discount, the lender gives up a number of percentage points in interest to reduce the rate and lower the payments for part of the mortgage term (usually for one year or less). After the discount period, the ARM rate usually increases according to its index rate.

down payment
Part of the purchase price of a property that is paid in cash and not financed with a mortgage.

effective gross income
Borrower's normal annual income, including overtime that is regular or guaranteed. Salary is usually the principal source, but other income may qualify if it is significant and stable.

equity
Amount of financial interest in a property. Equity is the difference between the fair market value of the property and the amount still owed on the mortgage.

escrow
Item(s) of value, money, or documents deposited with a third party to be delivered upon the fulfillment of a condition. For example, the deposit of funds or documents into an escrow account to be disbursed upon the closing of a sale of real estate.

escrow disbursements
Use of escrow funds to pay real estate taxes, hazard insurance, mortgage insurance, and other property expenses as they become due.

escrow payment
Part of a mortgagor's monthly payment that is held by the servicer to pay for taxes, hazard insurance, mortgage insurance, lease payments, and other items as they become due.

Fannie Mae
Congressionally chartered, shareholder-owned company that is the nation's largest supplier of home mortgage funds.

FHA mortgage
Mortgage that is insured by the Federal Housing Administration (FHA). Also known as a government mortgage.

FICO® score
FICO® scores are the most widely used credit score in U.S. mortgage loan underwriting. This three-digit number, ranging from 300 to 850, is calculated by a mathematical equation that evaluates many types of information that are on your credit report. Higher FICO® scores represent lower credit risks, which typically equate to better loan terms.

first mortgage
Primary lien against a property.

fixed installment
Monthly payment due on a mortgage loan including payment of both principal and interest.

fixed rate mortgage (FRM)
Mortgage with interest that remains the same throughout the entire term of the loan.

fully amortized ARM
Adjustable rate mortgage (ARM) with a monthly payment that is sufficient to amortize the remaining balance, at the interest accrual rate, over the amortization term.

GNMA ("Ginnie Mae")
Government-owned corporation that assumed responsibility for the special assistance loan program formerly administered by Fannie Mae.

growing-equity mortgage (GEM)
Fixed rate mortgage that provides scheduled payment increases over an established period of time. The increased amount of the monthly payment is applied directly toward reducing the remaining balance of the mortgage.

guarantee mortgage
Mortgage that is guaranteed by a third party.

housing expense ratio
Percentage of gross monthly income budgeted to pay housing expenses.

HUD-1 statement
Document that provides an itemized listing of the funds that are payable at closing. Items that appear on the statement include real estate commissions, loan fees, points, and initial escrow amounts. A separate number within a standardized numbering system represents each item on the statement. The totals at the

bottom of the HUD-1 statement define the seller's net proceeds and the buyer's net payment at closing.

hybrid ARM (3/1 ARM, 5/1 ARM, 7/1 ARM)
Combination fixed rate and adjustable rate loan—also called 3/1, 5/1, 7/1—can offer the best of both worlds. It has a lower interest rate (like an ARM) and a fixed payment for a longer period of time than most adjustable rate loans. For example, a "5/1 loan" has a fixed monthly payment and interest for the first five years and then turns into a traditional adjustable rate loan, based on then-current rates for the remaining 25 years. It's a good choice for people who expect to move or refinance before or shortly after the adjustment occurs.

index
Index is the measure of interest rate changes a lender uses to decide the amount an interest rate on an ARM will change over time. The index is generally a published number or percentage, such as the average interest rate or yield on Treasury bills. Some index rates tend to be higher than others and some are more volatile.

initial interest rate
Original interest rate of the mortgage at the time of closing. This rate changes for an adjustable rate mortgage (ARM). It's also called "start rate" or "teaser."

installment
Regular periodic payment that a borrower agrees to make to a lender.

insured mortgage
Mortgage that is protected by the Federal Housing Administration (FHA) or by private mortgage insurance (MI).

interest
Fee charged for borrowing money.

interest accrual rate
Percentage rate at which interest accrues on the mortgage. In most cases, it is also the rate used to calculate the monthly payments.

interest rate buy-down plan
Arrangement that allows the property seller to deposit money to an account. That money is then released each month to reduce the mortgagor's monthly payments during the early years of a mortgage.

interest rate ceiling
For an adjustable rate mortgage (ARM), the maximum interest rate, as specified in the mortgage note.

interest rate floor
For an adjustable rate mortgage (ARM), the minimum interest rate, as specified in the mortgage note.

late charge
Penalty a borrower must pay when a payment is made a stated number of days (usually 15) after the due date.

lease-purchase mortgage loan
Alternative financing option that allows low- and moderate-income homebuyers to lease a home with an option to buy. Each month's rent payment consists of principal, interest, taxes, and insurance (PITI) payments on the first mortgage plus an extra amount that accumulates in a savings account for a down payment.

liabilities
Person's financial obligation. Liabilities include long-term and short-term debt.

lifetime payment cap
For an adjustable rate mortgage (ARM), a limit on the amount that payments can increase or decrease over the life of the mortgage.

lifetime rate cap
For an adjustable-rate mortgage (ARM), this is a limit on the amount that the interest rate can increase or decrease over the life of the loan. *See* cap.

line of credit
Agreement by a commercial bank or other financial institution to extend credit up to a certain amount for a certain time.

liquid asset
Cash asset or an asset that is easily converted into cash.

loan
Borrowed money (principal) that is generally repaid with interest.

loan-to-value (LTV) percentage
Relationship between the principal balance of the mortgage and the appraised value (or sales price if it is lower) of the property. For example, a $100,000 home with an $80,000 mortgage has an LTV of 80%.

lock-in period
Specified period of time for which a specific interest rate is guaranteed by a lender, including loan term and points, if any, to be paid at closing. Short-term locks (under 21 days) are usually avail-

able after lender loan approval only. However, many lenders may permit a borrower to lock a loan for 30 days or more prior to submission of the loan application.

margin
Number of percentage points the lender adds to the index rate to calculate the ARM interest rate at each adjustment.

maturity
Date on which the principal balance of a loan becomes due and payable.

monthly fixed installment
Portion of the total monthly payment that is applied toward principal and interest. When a mortgage negatively amortizes, the monthly fixed installment does not include any amount for principal reduction and doesn't cover all of the interest. The loan balance therefore increases instead of decreasing.

mortgage
Legal document that pledges a property to the lender as security for payment of a debt.

mortgage banker
Company that originates mortgages exclusively for resale in the secondary mortgage market.

mortgage broker
Individual or company that brings borrowers and lenders together for the purpose of loan origination.

mortgage insurance
Contract that insures the lender against loss caused by a mortgagor's default on a government mortgage or conventional mort-

gage. Mortgage insurance can be issued by a private company or by a government agency.

mortgage insurance premium (MIP)
Amount paid by a mortgagor for mortgage insurance.

mortgage life insurance
Type of term life insurance. In the event that the borrower dies while the policy is in force the debt is automatically paid by insurance proceeds.

mortgagor
Borrower in a mortgage agreement.

negative amortization
Amortization means that monthly payments are large enough to pay the interest and reduce the principal on your mortgage. Negative amortization occurs when the monthly payments do not cover all of the interest cost. The interest cost that isn't covered is added to the unpaid principal balance. This means that even after making many payments, you could owe more than you did at the beginning of the loan. Negative amortization can occur when an ARM has a payment cap that results in monthly payments not high enough to cover the interest due.

net worth
Value of all of a person's assets, including cash.

non-liquid asset
Asset that cannot easily be converted into cash.

note
Legal document that obligates a borrower to repay a mortgage loan at a stated interest rate during a specified period of time.

origination fee
Fee paid to a lender for processing a loan application. The origination fee is stated in the form of points. One point is 1% of the mortgage amount.

owner financing
Property purchase transaction in which the party selling the property provides all or part of the financing.

payment change date
Date when a new monthly payment amount takes effect on an adjustable rate mortgage (ARM) or a graduated-payment mortgage (GPM). Generally, the payment change date occurs in the month immediately after the adjustment date.

periodic payment cap
Limit on the amount that payments can increase or decrease during any single adjustment period.

periodic rate cap
Limit on the amount that the interest rate can increase or decrease during any single adjustment period, regardless of how high or low the index might be.

PITI reserves
Cash amount that a borrower must have on hand after making a down payment and paying all closing costs for the purchase of a home. The principal, interest, taxes, and insurance (PITI) reserves must equal the amount that the borrower would have to pay for PITI for a predefined number of months (usually three).

point
One point is equal to 1% of the principal amount of your mortgage. For example, if you get a mortgage for $165,000, one point

means $1,650 to the lender. Points usually are collected at closing and may be paid by the borrower or the home seller, or may be split between them.

preapproval
Process of determining how much money you will be eligible to borrow before you apply for a loan.

prepayment penalty
Fee that may be charged to a borrower who pays off a loan before it is due.

prime rate
Interest rate that banks charge to their preferred customers. Changes in the prime rate influence changes in other rates, including mortgage interest rates.

principal
Amount borrowed or remaining unpaid. This is the part of the monthly payment that reduces the remaining balance of a mortgage.

principal balance
Outstanding balance of principal on a mortgage not including interest or any other charges.

principal, interest, taxes, and insurance (PITI)
The four components of a monthly mortgage payment. Principal refers to the part of the monthly payment that reduces the remaining balance of the mortgage. Interest is the fee charged for borrowing money. Taxes and insurance refer to the monthly costs of property taxes and homeowners insurance, whether these amounts are paid into an escrow account each month or not.

private mortgage insurance (PMI)
Mortgage insurance provided by a private mortgage insurance company to protect lenders against loss if a borrower defaults. Most lenders generally require mortgage insurance for a loan with a loan-to-value (LTV) percentage in excess of 80%.

qualified intermediary
A qualified intermediary acts as an independent third party to ensure safe harbor in a 1031 Exchange. Like Kind Exchanges involve business or investment property that is exchanged for like kind property. Like Kind Exchanges must not involve constructive receipt of cash for the property relinquished. So the use of a qualified intermediary can facilitate the exchange using escrow accounts. The particular intermediary promises to return the proceeds of the exchange to the transferor of the property.

qualifying ratios
Calculations used to determine whether a borrower qualifies for a mortgage. They consist of two separate calculations: a housing expense as a percent of income ratio and total debt obligations as a percent of income ratio.

rate lock
A commitment issued by a lender to a borrower or other mortgage originator guaranteeing a specified interest rate and lender costs for a specified period of time.

real estate agent
Person licensed to negotiate and transact the sale of real estate on behalf of the property owner.

Real Estate Settlement Procedures Act (RESPA)
Consumer protection law that requires lenders to give borrowers advance notice of closing costs.

Realtor®
Real estate broker or an associate who is an active member in a local real estate board that is affiliated with the National Association of Realtors.

recording
The noting in the registrar's office of the details of a properly executed legal document, such as a deed, a mortgage note, a satisfaction of mortgage, or an extension of mortgage, thereby making it a part of the public record.

refinancing
Paying off one loan with the proceeds from a new loan using the same property as security.

revolving liability
Credit arrangement, such as a credit card, that allows a customer to borrow against a preapproved line of credit when purchasing goods and services.

secondary mortgage market
Where existing mortgages are bought and sold.

security
Property that will be pledged as collateral for a loan.

seller carry-back
Agreement in which the owner of a property provides financing, often in combination with an assumable mortgage. *See* owner financing.

servicer
Organization that collects principal and interest payments from borrowers and manages borrowers' escrow accounts. The servicer

often services mortgages that have been purchased by an investor in the secondary mortgage market.

standard payment calculation
Method used to determine the monthly payment required to repay the remaining balance of a mortgage in substantially equal installments over the remaining term of the mortgage at the current interest rate.

step-rate mortgage
Mortgage that allows for the interest rate to increase according to a specified schedule (i.e., seven years), resulting in increased payments as well. At the end of the specified period, the rate and payments will remain constant for the remainder of the loan. Also called "graduated-rate mortgage (GRM)."

third-party origination
Use by the lender of another party to completely or partially originate, process, underwrite, close, fund, or package the mortgages it plans to deliver to the secondary mortgage market.

total expense ratio
Total obligations as a percentage of gross monthly income including monthly housing expenses plus other monthly debts.

Treasury Index
Index used to determine interest rate changes for certain adjustable-rate mortgage (ARM) plans. It is based on the results of auctions that the U.S. Treasury holds for its Treasury bills and securities or derived from the U.S. Treasury's daily yield curve, which in turn is based on the closing market bid yields on actively traded Treasury securities in the over-the-counter market.

Truth-in-Lending Act
Federal law that requires lenders to fully disclose, in writing, the terms and conditions of a mortgage, including the annual percentage rate (APR) and other charges.

two-step mortgage
Adjustable rate mortgage (ARM) with one interest rate for the first five or seven years of its mortgage term and a different interest rate for the remainder of the amortization term.

underwriting
Process of evaluating a loan application to determine the risk involved for the lender. Underwriting involves an analysis of the borrower's creditworthiness and the quality of the property itself.

VA mortgage
Mortgage that is guaranteed by the Department of Veterans Affairs (VA). Also known as a "government mortgage."

"wraparound" mortgage
A mortgage that includes the remaining balance on an existing first mortgage plus an additional amount requested by the mortgagor. Full payments on both mortgages are made to the "wraparound" mortgagee, who then forwards the payments on the first mortgage to the first mortgagee. These mortgages may not be allowed by the first mortgage holder, and if discovered, could be subject to a demand for full payment.

Index

About the Authors

Anthony Cutaia has over 35 years of diverse experience in the financial markets. He began his career as a stockbroker and registered investment advisor, and has developed residential and commercial real estate properties valued at over $120 million.

Founder and chief executive officer of the Boca Raton, Florida–based Cutaia Mortgage Group Inc., he started his career 35 years ago as a stockbroker and registered investment advisor. But handling deals for other investors wasn't enough for him: He yearned to invest for his own account—to act upon the creative and innovative ideas *he* had for developing and investing in real estate. So he founded A.F. Cutaia & Co., a real estate investment and development company with offices on Madison Avenue in New York City. His wife Susan was a partner in the family-owned company.

After choosing to relocate the business to the more lucrative real estate market in Florida, Anthony went into the mortgage business, earning a mortgage broker's license.

Susan and Anthony are the creators and hosts of "Talk About Mortgages and Real Estate," a successful live call-in educational radio and television program heard daily and viewed weekly by over 4 million South Floridians.

The show, nine years old, can be heard on WSBR and WNN Radio, and seen on the NBC affiliate, WPTV News Channel 5, with a potential viewership of 1.3 million, focusing on the West Palm Beach market. It can also be seen on WPXP-TV, which reaches a potential viewership of 3.1 million from Boca Raton to Vero Beach.

The show airs daily, and addresses the ins and outs of Florida's fast-paced real estate market, targeting the early to sophisticated investor, and educating listeners on how the right mortgage instrument can be used as a tool for wealth creation.

Susan and Anthony and are also the real estate and mortgage editors respectively for News 12's "South Florida Business Report," the longest-running local business news program in South Florida, which airs at 8:30 AM Sundays on WPEC News 12.

The Cutaias also host free monthly investment seminars, which average 100 visitors. They have also held paid investment seminars that draw an average of 500 people.

In 2001, Anthony and Susan founded Cutaia Mortgage Group Inc., a licensed mortgage brokerage business and correspondent lender. Cutaia Mortgage now boasts over 20 employees and 45 mortgage brokers; it has a branch office in Delray Beach.

Anthony launched Cutaia Title and Abstract LLC in 2005, a firm that provides title searches and title insurance for those purchasing and refinancing real estate properties run by his attorney daughter Dawn Cutaia-Watchilla. He also opened Cutaia Realty Advisors LLC, a full-service real estate brokerage firm specializing in commercial real estate transactions. The newest member of the Cutaia family is Cutaia Real Estate Institute LLC, launched in March 2006.

Anthony is a licensed mortgage broker, real estate broker, and real estate instructor in the State of Florida.

He was named the top mortgage broker for the State of Florida by *Broker Magazine* in 2005.

Susan Cutaia is president of Cutaia Mortgage Group, Inc.

She grew up in New York City, where she graduated from Forest Hills High School. Soon after graduation, she married Anthony Cutaia, and later raised their four children: Dawn, Diana, Elizabeth, and Anthony in Bronxville, New York, and Greenwich, Connecticut. The Cutaias have been married for over 40 years, and reside in Boca Raton, Florida.

Susan has over 40 years of business experience, having worked at Warner Lambert and J.C. Penney Co. After relocating to Boca Raton, where the Cutaia family maintained a second home, Susan served as president of National Sales Marketing, a firm that imported and exported safety and security products, from 1991 through 1996.

In 1996, Susan joined a mortgage lender in Boca Raton as a loan officer, where she teamed up with her husband, Anthony. They quickly became the firm's top revenue producers.

Susan is a licensed mortgage broker in New York and Florida. She is the Past President of the Boca/Delray chapter of the National Association of Women Business Owners (NAWBO), and Past Treasurer of the State NAWBO. Susan also served as an elected delegate to the White House Conference on Small Business.

Robert Slater has written 18 books on major business personalities, including Bill Gates, Donald Trump, and Martha Stewart. His books, *Jack Welch and the GE Way*, and *SOROS: The Life, Times, and Trading Secrets of the World's Greatest Investor*, were *BusinessWeek* best sellers.